Glitter and Glue

Also by Kelly Corrigan:

The Middle Place
Lift

Glitter and Glue

A memoir

Kelly Corrigan

CORONET

First published in Great Britain in 2013 by Coronet
An imprint of Hodder & Stoughton
An Hachette UK company

First published in paperback in 2015

1

A CIP catalogue record for this title is available from the British Library

ISBN 978 1 444 72515 5
Ebook ISBN 978 1 444 72516 2

Printed and bound by Clays Ltd, St Ives plc

Hodder & Stoughton policy is to use papers that are natural,
renewable and recyclable products and made from wood grown
in sustainable forests. The logging and manufacturing processes
are expected to conform to the environmental regulations
of the country of origin.

Hodder & Stoughton Ltd
338 Euston Road
London NW1 3BH

www.hodder.co.uk

For the yearbook, the fifth-graders at Havens Elementary are asked to name the one person they most admire. Finley Swan said, "My mom!" So did that sweet Madeline Malan. My daughter put "Tom Brady." The football player.

This one's for you, Ma. Long overdue.

Author's Note

This is a work of memory, and mine is as flawed and biased as any other. I was aided by dozens of old letters, photographs, journals (both mine and my friend Tracy's), and the Internet, on which I could call up images of just about everywhere I went in 1992. Many of the names and personal details have been changed.

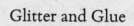

Glitter and Glue

Prologue

When I was growing up, my mom was guided by the strong belief that to befriend me was to deny me the one thing a kid really needed to survive childhood: a mother. Consequently, we were never one of those Mommy & Me pairs who sat close or giggled. She didn't wink at me or gush about how pretty I looked or rub my back to help me fall asleep. She was not a big fan of deep conversation, and she still doesn't go for a lot of physical contact. She looked at motherhood less as a joy to be relished than as a job to be done, serious work with serious repercussions, and I left childhood assuming our way of being with each other, adversarial but functional, was as it would be.

If my mother thought of me as someone to guide, my father thought of me as someone to cheer. I was his girl, as in *That's my girl! Have you met my girl?* He liked to hold hands and high-five and was almost impossible to frustrate or disappoint. His signature *You bet! Why not?* energy was all I needed for several decades. But then my daily life became more consequential, and I woke up needing things he could not supply—a certain understanding, call it a seasoning—that only my mother seemed to have. Her areas of expertise, which often had appeared piddling or immaterial, became disturbingly relevant. And that's saying nothing about the second-guessing and anxieties I could take to her, worries that would only ever bounce off my dad's optimism, as was the case on the day I was told I needed surgery.

I remember leaving the doctor thinking three things:

I can't have more kids.

It's for my own good.

I need my mom.

On the way to the parking lot, I dialed home or, I should say, the place that was home when I was a child. My dad ran to pick up the phone on the first ring. I know because I've seen him do it a hundred times. He loves connecting, he's dying to catch up, can't wait to hear your voice, anyone's voice.

"Lovey!" he sang out, as if it had been years, not days, since we talked. "How's my girl?"

"I'm okay. Is Mom there?" I wasn't crying, but I wanted to.

"What?" he said in mock hysteria. "You don't want to talk to Greenie? The Green Man?" My dad's brothers have been calling him Greenie since college. I always thought it referred to the Irish in him, but it turns out it's more about a bad hangover. "You're breaking my heart, Lovey!"

"Sorry. I just need Mom."

"She's at the bridge table, probably making her opponents weep right this minute!"

I asked him to have her call me when she got back, and told him I couldn't talk right now. That was A-OK with him, because everything is A-OK with him.

"Love ya, mean it," he signed off, as usual.

"Love ya, mean it."

Before I got in my car, I called my mom's cell and left a message explaining that Dr. Rawson would be taking out my ovaries a week from Thursday. I tried to sound cool and relaxed about it. I said I was being spayed, ha ha. I hoped she would hear past my witty BS.

Two years before, a lump I found in my breast turned out to be a seven-centimeter tumor. So I did what people with tumors do: chemotherapy, radiation, surgery. I also started taking a tiny pill every day to suppress ovarian function, since my cancer used estrogen to multiply. After ninety days, my periods kept coming. I bragged to the doc that I was born to breed. Turned out there was something on my ovary—a cyst, most likely—but it did not wax and wane, the way cysts should. It sat there, stubborn and ominous. The time had come.

"You have kids?" the doctor asked.

"Yeah, two girls. Three and five."

"We do this now, and maybe we avoid something worse later."

Crossing the Bay Bridge, San Francisco disappearing behind me, I did not call my husband. Edward was a reasonable man who took zinc at the first sign of a cold, stretched thoroughly before and after exercise, and, when lifting heavy objects, used his legs, not his back. He was, in all situations, an advocate for avoiding something worse.

I did not call either of my older brothers, I do not have a sister, and I was not quite ready to involve a girlfriend. So I called my mom's cell again, and this time she answered. She said she'd just hung up with *the idiot at the airlines* who wouldn't accept her frequent-flier miles, which were *barely* expired, and I said, "God help the customer service guy who took that call," but what I thought was *She's coming*.

She arrived from Philly the day before I went in for surgery, letting Edward carry her tiny black suitcase on wheels up the stairs, where she would unpack all her must-haves: a silk pillowcase that keeps her hairdo looking nice, her mauve bathrobe with giant pearly buttons, a small jelly jar of Smirnoff because she doesn't like the expensive vodka we buy, and several strange secondhand presents—a bedazzled purse, one of my old Nancy Drews, a down vest with a broken zipper—for the girls. Georgia and Claire love her and always have. She's different with them. She makes Jell-O—*a hundred percent sugar-free, Kelly*—and plays Crazy Eights and rubs lotion on their clean feet and reads them whatever they bring to her, even the long books with no pictures. When she leaves them, she cries. Actually cries, with real tears. From a woman who extended the adage *Children should be seen and not heard* with *and preferably not seen,* it's startling, like opening your toolbox and discovering that your supposedly industrial-strength staples are made of Play-Doh.

After the procedure, Edward brought me home, where everything was fine and good and just the same but somehow different. The girls gave me homemade cards with words my mom helped them spell, like *operation* and *recovery*. I showed them my bandage. Then Edward said, "All right, ladies, the day is done. Up we go."

The next morning, Edward dropped the girls at school on the way to work while I lay in bed and listened to my mom talk on the phone to my dad. "Make sure to check the leak in the basement . . . and call the dry cleaners and tell them they overcharged us . . . She's doing well . . . the girls are divine . . . All right, will do."

I was in bed, not wanting to ask her to come sit with me but still listening for her footsteps on the stairs.

After a while, she called up, "Need anything from Florence Nightingale?"

"The newspaper, or some company, maybe."

She grabbed the railing and made her way up to me.

We talked about my new comforter cover, how I got it on sale because of one tiny tear. *Good for you.*

I told her a story about Claire not wanting to get older because then she would have to move out and live far away. *That Claire.*

She swore she was going to quit selling real estate one of these days. *My God, it's been twenty years.*

We rolled our eyes about my dad and how he plans his life around the Radnor High School lacrosse schedule and then acknowledged how good the kids from the team have been, coming to clean the gutters in the fall and shovel the driveway after it snows. *Anything for Coach Corrigan.*

I asked her when I should look at my scars, and she said, *Never.* She said she hasn't looked at her naked stomach since the sixties, when it was still flat and unstretched.

We kept up the chitchat, never breaking the rhythm of our conversational song because it had been a long two years of thinking hard thoughts, and my mom doesn't like that crap.

"Well, I'm gonna let you sleep," she decided, pulling the string that dropped my shade and muttering about the pulley and how she can never get the *damn thing* to release.

"You know who I think about?" I said, sensing that our time was almost up. "That lady, the mom in Australia, Ellen Tanner."

"Oh, honey." She stopped and turned and leaned on the end of my bed. "Don't think about her. That's not going to happen to you."

"I know. She's just—on my mind sometimes." I didn't say any more. It would have cracked me open. Anyway, the thing was, my mom knew who I was talking about and why, and she called me *honey* and promised that I was going to be okay and that was what I needed and she knew it so I was good.

If you had asked me, after I graduated from college, whose voice I would hear in my head for the rest of my life, whose voice I would want to hear, I'd have said some combination of my dad's and my roommate Tracy's and Jackson Browne's. I would have continued with ten or twenty or two hundred others before I got to my mom. But now, give me almost any situation—termites, refinancing or back pain, allowance, mean girls or sibling rivalry, a child's despair, a husband's inattention, or my own spikes of rage and regret—and watch how fast I dial her number.

The fact is, lately it seems like the only person who can lift the anvils that sit heaviest on me is my mother. It didn't happen all at once. Maybe it was inevitable, something that develops as daily life delivers its sucker punches, streaks of clarity, and slow-dawning wisdoms. But I know when it started: twenty years ago, in the home of Ellen Tanner, a woman I never met.

PART ONE

1992

I shouldn't be here. That's what I'm realizing as I follow John Tanner down the hall of his house in suburban Australia. After the interview, I should've called back and said it wasn't going to work. But I had no choice. I needed money, or I'd be back on my mother's doorstep within a month, and wouldn't that please her to no end?

It's her fault. That's another thought I'm having as I set down my backpack on a single bed in a room with a skylight but no windows, and John Tanner says, "I hope this will be okay." If she had given me even a little money . . . a loan . . .

This is not what I left home for. That's the chalky horse pill I choke down when John Tanner says the kids are so excited about me moving in, they'll be in here bouncing on my bed in no time. "First nanny and all," he says.

I'm a nanny, a fucking nanny.

For the record, I didn't touch down in Oz, open *The Sydney Morning Herald,* and circle "Recent Widower Looking for Live-in Nanny." If anything, I was thinking bartending, or at least waitressing. Good money, tons of laughs, guys everywhere.

My college roommate Tracy and I had been traveling for two months, burning through cash, so when we got off the bus in downtown Sydney, we filled out applications at all the restaurants and bars that sounded Yank-friendly: Uncle Sam's, Texas

Rib Joint, New York Steak House. We followed up, we waited. Seven days in, we broadened the search—surf shacks, burger joints, cafés, pubs. Nobody would hire us. We called friends of friends and left messages asking if they knew of any temp work. No one called us back. We tried all the bulletins posted at the hostels. No one would bend the rules to let us work under the table. So after three weeks, we did what no self-respecting globe-trotter would: We looked in the help-wanted ads for nanny gigs, all of which were in the 'burbs, where we would meet zero boys and have zero big experiences and learn nothing about anything.

I picked a rich family with an indoor pool and views of the Sydney Opera House, but Eugenia Brown turned out to be a total despot, and after I made a funny face about scrubbing her pool tiles and dragged my heels about helping with a mailing regarding her availability as a bridge tutor, I pointed out that her ad had said nanny, not nanny *plus* housecleaner *plus* personal assistant, at which point she said I was her first American—she usually hired Asians, who had "worked out so nicely"—and that I might be too "unionized." Then she fired me.

After that, I interviewed with four more families. I told Smiley Vicki in Chatswood that I was open to babysitting on weekend nights, which would suck, and Skinny Jane on Cove Lane that I knew CPR. Didn't matter. No one wanted a nanny who could only stay for five months, so I went back to the newspaper, and the widower's ad was still there.

John Tanner was older than I thought a man with a seven-year-old and a five-year-old would be. His mustache was graying, and his hairline had rolled back a touch from where it started. His shoulders were sloped, giving him the outline of my grandmother's Frigidaire. All in all, he struck me as someone who might participate in Civil War reenactments.

In a conversation that lasted under an hour, he explained that he was a steward for Qantas and used to work the overnights to New Zealand, Tokyo, and Singapore. It had been more than six months since his wife passed, and it was time to resume his usual schedule. He needed an extra pair of hands, someone who could drive the kids to school when he was flying. He didn't care that I couldn't commit to a year. He couldn't either. He said this would be a good way to test the nanny plan—he wasn't sure it was the right long-term solution for them—and I said that sounds great to me, and we shook hands, the deal done. He did not ask to make a copy of my passport. He was tired and I was good enough for now.

The house is a rancher half-painted in such an ill-chosen orange—probably called "Happy Face" or "Sunny Outlook"—that I wonder if he's color-blind, or relied on his wife for those sorts of decisions. Gallon cans, half unopened, line the porch. There's no discernible method to the painting, just halfhearted swaths of color here and there. The patches under the windows make it look like the house itself is crying.

In the living room, John's widowhood is even more evident. There's crayon on the walls and puzzle pieces sprinkled on the floor. The sofa's slipcover is bunched up. On the side table, a plastic dinosaur is tipped over in rigor mortis beside a framed school photo of a girl in a plaid uniform, pushed back against a small treasure chest you might get from a dentist or a fast-food restaurant. A piano bench overflows with drawings on pages that, I see as I get closer, are sheet music. *Tilt,* I hear my mother say, which I believe refers to the message pinball machines flash when players lose control, but I can't say for sure. Some of her expressions are hard to deconstruct. (I learned only recently that when she says *Mikey!* after the first bite of something good, she's alluding to the old Life cereal commercial.)

My bag unpacked, John's son, Martin, trots toward me on the balls of his feet like a show pony. He's scrawny, and his ears rise to a point, like the Texan Ross Perot, who just announced his campaign for president.

"Keely!" he calls, his accent lifting the middle of my name until it rhymes with *wheelie*. I met him only briefly during the interview last week, but that's no matter to him. We're friends already.

"Hello there!"

His smile is loose and wavy, and his lips have a line of red crust along the edges from too much licking. I have lip balm in my pocket. I could start fixing him right now.

"Listen!" he says. I watch as he bangs around on the piano, creating a soaring anthem of madness and joy before spinning around to check my reaction, making me feel important.

"Brilliant. Bravo! Do it again!" I say, clapping. He whips back around, raises his hands high in the air, and pauses like a pelican hovering over an unsuspecting fish. "Go!" I say.

He drops his hands to the keys in a free fall and hammers out a near cousin to his first composition.

"Genius. Pure—"

"LOUD RUBBISH," Milly, who would hardly look at me when we met, hollers from the TV room. "I'M TRYING TO WATCH MY SHOW!"

"I can play! Keely wants me to play!"

"Well, I don't!" she shouts. "Daddy!"

"OY!" John silences the two of them. All three of us, actually.

I peek around the corner to make nice with Milly, who sits

low in a chair, wearing her school uniform: a plaid kilt with a thin white shirt, untucked. Her lips are pressed together, her hands tucked under her thighs. If she could make herself disappear into the crease of the chair, she would. She has a round face, a dozen freckles sprinkled across each cheek, blue eyes, and thick sandy hair gilded with highlights that a middle-aged woman would pay a lot for.

"Hello," I say.

"Hi," she says, barely moving her lips.

"So, you're coming up on eight, right? Wow!" She looks at me like, *Really? Is it really so "wow"?* Her fingernail polish is chipped. I have a bottle of polish in my bag. I could fix her, too. "What grade are you in again?"

She doesn't answer.

"Amelia Tanner, Kelly is asking you a question," John prods from the kitchen.

"Second."

"What are you watching?"

"Television." *Little Miss Smart-mouth,* I hear my mom say.

"Do you like hard candy?" I hold out a lemon drop.

"No. Thank you." Her accent brings to mind the British Royals, as do her robotic manners. She doesn't want a nanny. She knows how it is that her family has come to need the help of Some Lady. She knows I'm here to help everyone Transition. Even if no one else cares that a stranger will soon be making her sandwiches, zipping her jacket, and signing her permission slips on the line clearly marked *Parent's Signature,* her loyalty is with her mother, wherever she is.

"What's your name?" Martin says, appearing behind me holding a big encyclopedic book called *Marsupials.*

"You know my name, silly. Kelly."

"What's your mum's name?" he asks innocently. I glance over at Milly, who doesn't seem to be disturbed by his question.

"Um, Mary."

"What's your name?"

"Kelly."

"What's your mum's name?" he says again, in the very same cheery tone that, mercifully, undercuts what otherwise would be an unbearably sad call-and-response.

"Mary."

I look to Milly for help, but she's busy transmitting her distrust using only her eyes: *Don't think you can come in here and take over just because you're all buddy-buddy with my chump brother.* She will not be diverted by my cheer and candy. She will not throw open the gates to the territory and stand by while I tromp all over their sacred ground.

Well guess what, Milly Tanner? I don't want to be here, either. I didn't save for a year and fly halfway across the world to stir-fry kangaroo meat and pick up your "skivvies" off the bathroom floor. This was supposed to be my trip of a lifetime, my Technicolor dream.

Things happen when you leave the house. That's my motto. I made it up on an Outward Bound trip after college. During the Solo—three days and three nights alone on a stretch of beach in the Florida Everglades with a tent, five gallons of water, an apple, an orange, and a first-aid kit—I made the most of what my hairy vegan counselor, Jane, called "a singular opportunity to plan your life."

After deciding where to put my tent, dragging my water into a patch of shade, floating naked and singing "I Will Survive" by Gloria Gaynor, I pulled out my journal and mapped out my life in yearly, sometimes monthly, increments. No way was I going to be just another apple rotting at the base of my mother's tree. I was going to roll. I was going to Do Things Worth Doing and Know Things Worth Knowing. Seventy-two hours later, when Jane pulled up in the motorboat, all major decisions were settled: work, grad school, relationships, moves, marriage, childbearing. I went all the way up to my death, a peaceful event that I scheduled for 2057.

But for all my zealous imagining, a year later I looked up from my life and was deeply unimpressed. I worked at the bottom rung of a nonprofit in downtown Baltimore, and thanks to the understandably pitiful pay, I lived with Libby, my grandmother on my mom's side, which meant that except for Tuesdays, when I had Weight Watchers, I spent every weeknight eating roasted meats and Pillsbury dinner rolls with Libby and her very crazy brother, whom everyone called Uncle Slug. By eight o'clock on any given night, I was up in my room—the room where my great-great-aunt Gerty lived until she died in the rocking chair that still sat by the window—highlighting *The Seven Habits of Highly Effective People* until my next move became clear.

If I really wanted to grow, well, that was not going to happen while I was living with my granny, driving my shit Honda two miles to the office every day, clocking in to happy hour on Water Street at five P.M., hoping some club lacrosse player would try to suck my face behind the phone booth after pounding a Jägermeister shot. I needed to get out. I needed an adventure. So I found a round-the-world ticket on sale in the back of *The New York Times* and talked Tracy into coming with me. One year, seven countries, bang-o—odyssey!

When I laid out the plan for my parents, my dad said, "Lovey, FANTASTIC!" He would know. He went to Australia with a lacrosse team back in the late fifties. "Go get 'em, Lovey!" He's a Life Eater, my dad.

My mom said, "You haven't been out of college two years yet. You need to focus on making money, saving up."

"I *have* saved. How do you think I'm paying for the plane ticket?"

"You should be using that money to get established, get your own health insurance, not traipse all over creation," she said. "I certainly hope you're not expecting help from your father and me."

"I'm not." (Hoping, maybe.)

"Good. You don't want to come home to a mountain of debt."

"Mom, I get it."

"You get it. I bet you get it," she said, mostly to herself, as she cut a sliver of lemon rind to toss in her five o'clock drink.

"Anyway, I'll go back to work when I get home."

"You better hope they'll take you back."

"They will."

She looked at me like I thought I knew everything. "You really think you know everything, don't you?"

"Here's what I know: I want Life Experience!"

"You know what's good Life Experience? Life. Real life is excellent life experience," she said, pleased with her retort. "How does running around Australia apply to anything . . . like working, marriage, family?"

"Mom—God! You know what? Things happen when you leave the house."

"What?"

"I'm not going to magically become interesting sitting on

the sofa. I'm not going to learn anything—my values, or purpose, or point of view—at home. Things happen when you *leave*, when you walk out the door, up the driveway, and into the world."

"I don't know why you don't walk out the door and go to an office, like everyone else."

Despite my mom's total failure to get behind me, I liked everything about the odyssey plan. I even liked the vocabulary of travel: distant shores, exotic vistas, excursions, expeditions. Show me the poetry in *ground-beef special, informational interview, staff development.*

Two months later, my parents walked me to the gate at JFK. I spotted Tracy from a hundred yards away—she's six feet, a head taller than all the Taiwanese in line for our flight to Taipei—with her mom. They have the same haircut because they go to the same hairdresser; they share clothes and shoes, sunglasses and jewelry, which they can do because Tracy's mom has pierced ears, like a normal person. My mom wears clip-ons that feel like little vises on my earlobes.

As my parents and I approached, Tracy and her mom started their goodbye. They said *I love you* and *I love you, too* and *Have the time of your life!* They kissed and hugged, and when they pulled apart, they both had tears in their eyes, which made them laugh the exact same laugh at the exact same moment.

My mom stood in front of me with her pleather pocketbook snuggled cautiously under one arm.

"All right, now," she said, "be very careful with your passport and your travelers' checks." She had said this ten times in the last two weeks.

"I know, Mom," I said, putting my arms around her. We patted each other, and then she released.

When my dad stepped forward, my mom looked away.

"Lovey, go get 'em, kid!" I bear-hugged my dad. We rocked back and forth.

"Here, girls," my mom said, handing Tracy and me each a neon-green pack of gum from her extra-valu pak. "For your ears, on the descent."

"Thanks," we said.

"What a pair!" my dad said as we headed to the gate.

We turned around one more time before we disappeared into our whale of a future. My mom had her arms crossed and her lips pursed as if she'd just lost an argument and couldn't quite believe it, but then my dad put his arm around her, and I heard his booming voice say, "Aw, Mare, she's gonna be fine," and I thought, *Greenie, you've got it all wrong. She never once said anything about being* worried.

I assumed the whole trip would be like Bangkok, where even crossing the street was an adventure. Seven or eight lanes of cars pushing around on a highway built for four, the side-walks jammed with fruit sellers and fish stands, sacks of spices, nuts, and dried meats. Even the alphabet was overflowing: forty-four consonants and fourteen vowels. Plus, they didn't have toilets. We had to squat over holes. My mom would have died.

After a couple of days getting organized, Tracy and I took an all-night bus to a ferry to an island. Onshore, we were mauled by bungalow operators waving photos and calling, *Lady, lady, this way, come this way*. Along with a couple from Stockholm and a boy from Crete, we picked a place called Bun-galow Bill's because the guy said, *Plumbing, good plumbing*. As soon as we got in his tuk-tuk, a makeshift motor cart, I started taking pictures even though it wasn't safe or convenient. I had to have proof.

At Bungalow Bill's, we had beers with this guy Joe, who was much older, like thirty. He'd been all over—Burma, Sri Lanka, Bhutan. He had no idea where he was going next or for how long. *I just go*, he said, establishing himself as Person of Interest #1.

When we told him we were going from Thailand to Australia, he said we were crazy to miss Indonesia. He said we could spend months traveling from island to island, seeing temples and volcanoes, estuaries and coral reefs. We told him our flight wasn't flexible like that; we couldn't fly to Jakarta without paying some kind of penalty. He said we'd never be this close to so many places, and we needed to be awake to the possibilities, which instantly became my mantra.

Tracy and I went back and forth about Indonesia. We called the airlines and looked at guidebooks and talked to other travelers. In the end, we couldn't stomach the rerouting fee, so we boarded the plane, as planned, to Australia, settling in for six hours of Merit Ultra Lights and backgammon on the tiny magnetized board that Tracy's mom had given us as a bon voyage gift. After dinner and three mini-bottles of Chardonnay, totally free, Tracy went to sleep, her legs folded up against the seat in front of her like a giraffe in a phone booth, while I wrote in my journal about how, when we got to Australia, we needed to totally Go for It at every crossroad, by which I did not ever mean that we should become nannies.

But here I am, saving up, trying to somehow Be Awake to the Possibilities in a neighborhood that's basically indistinguishable from the one where I grew up. Three- and four-bedroom houses with bikes on the lawn and potted plants by the front door. Dads jumping in cars by eight A.M., moms in bathrobes dashing out to grab the newspaper to see what the rest of the world did yesterday, and kids on swing sets, oblivious to it all. Some exotic vista.

A month ago, I was the curious American in the Thai hostel, confabbing with Greeks and Swedes and Buddhists fresh from the ashram. Now I'm the weird new appendage hanging off the sagging mobile that is the Tanner family.

That first afternoon, before we sit down for dinner, Martin appears at my door, holding out three toy dinosaurs. "They're mine, but you can have them."

"Oh, wow, thanks. I'll just borrow them."

"Okay," he says. "For how long?"

"Well, for as long as they like it in here."

He sets them carefully on my bedside shelf. "They'll like it in here. It's dark. They like the dark. They're never scared."

"Do they have names?"

"T. rex, Barosaurus . . ."

I meant name-names like Pete or maybe something Australian like Baz or Norbert but now I see that a boy can hardly find a better word to say, a word that confers more authority, than Ve-lo-ci-rap-tor.

"They're from the Crustinsashus Period," he says with pride.

"One of my favorites."

"Really?"

"Totally."

"Martin, dinner. Keely, too," Milly calls from the kitchen, her voice sharp.

"Come on, Keely!" Martin says, holding out his hand. "See how my daddy can cook now."

Dinner is ham and cheese on brown bread with some chips.

None of it looks good to me, but I eat it all, because I'm a guest or, God help me, a role model. This would amuse my mother. It's just the sort of mundane shit she wanted me to be worrying about.

"How long have you lived here?" I ask John as he moves Martin's milk away from the edge of the table.

"Since Ellen and I got mar— Martin, put your napkin in your lap," John says. Milly leans over and pushes Martin's napkin onto his thighs. "For a while now, eight years. I guess actually nine." I can't tell whether this last year hardly registers or counts double. Maybe he can't even remember it, maybe it's all there is.

Milly eats every chip and then sits back in her chair.

"Eat your sandwich," John says, tapping the table in front of her.

"I don't like the cheese."

"Take it off, then."

"I don't like the ham."

"Amelia—"

She looks over at me, waiting to see if I will insert myself, which I will not.

"I'm not hun—"

"Now."

She picks up her sandwich and takes a mousy bite, fake-chewing, reminding me of all the ways I found not to eat whatever awfulness my mother forced on me (bread crust, spaghetti sauce, dark meat) when I was Milly's age.

As Milly stares at her sandwich, Martin runs his fingers around the outside of his, working the excess mayonnaise like a bricklayer does mortar.

John smacks the table with his open hand. "No fingers!"

Martin looks down as Milly takes another bite, bravely, like a soldier taking stitches in the field.

"Daddy—" Milly points at her brother, who is rolling his greasy hands around in his T-shirt.

"Martin! Use your serviette! And apologize to Kelly."

To me? What do I have to do with any of this?

Martin apologizes without hesitation or, for that matter, feeling.

After a period of terrible silence, uneaten sandwiches disassembled on plates, John leans back, exhales, and says, "Who wants ice cream?" *Ice cream?* I hear my mother say. *After that behavior?*

"We do!"

"With toppings!"

So, John, who just moments ago was beside himself with frustration, heads to the kitchen to dole out treats. *Someone needs a little backbone,* my mother whispers.

While the kids are busy with their jimmies and chocolate sauce, John tells me about Pop, who lives in an in-law unit attached to the house. Pop is eighty-four. Pop lived most of his life in Fiji. Pop is a widower, too. He keeps to himself and is no trouble, and I am not expected to worry about him for meals or anything at all. He came over a couple of years ago, when Ellen first started chemo, and now he'll probably stay.

Milly lifts her head from her ice cream. "Probably?"

"As long as he wants," John assures her, committing to house the father of his dead wife indefinitely.

"He likes it here. Like the dinosaurs," Martin whispers to me.

"I see," I say, thinking less about Pop and the dinosaurs and more about John saying that Ellen was in chemo. I didn't know it was cancer. It didn't come up in the interview, and I didn't have the guts to ask.

"And then there's Evan, Ellen's son from her first marriage, who lives in a room off the garage. He's in and out, he won't bother you." How had Evan and Pop not come up before?

Martin announces he's done. *Finished,* my mom corrects. *Meat is done. Are you a slab of meat?*

After dessert, I start to clear the table, but John shoos me away, saying I must be tired, and I take the opening to say good night.

Stretching out on the bed, I rotate my thoughts like a camera on a tripod, away from the Tanner kids and malignancies to the reason I am here. On a clean two-page spread in my journal, I make the official list of all the Life Eating I'm going to do, starting five months from today.

Hiking/Waterfalls—Radical Bay
Sailing—Whitsunday Islands
Camping—Fraser Island
Ayers Rock
Rain Forest—Cape Tribulation
Horseback Riding
Scuba Dive—Great Barrier Reef
Bungee Jump—Queenstown
Fjords—New Zealand
Fox Glacier
Beach Time/Island Hopping—Fiji

I sit back and stare at the list. THIS IS IT, I write at the bottom in all capital letters. THIS IS IT!

The next morning, I'm alone in the kitchen, watching myself make a cup of tea from somewhere outside my body, wondering what I am doing here, when John Tanner appears in the doorway wearing sweatpants and a T-shirt. He's no Val Kilmer, but I could sort of imagine that with a good haircut, some jogging, more color in his cheeks—I don't know, maybe he could be made over and sent back out there.

"Sleep okay?" he asks.

"Yes, thanks. You?"

He shrugs as if he long ago abandoned expectations about things like sleep. "Is that coffee?"

"Tea. I can make coff—"

"No. No worries." He lumbers over to a drawer and digs around for filters.

"Should I wake up the kids?"

"Sure."

When I get back there, Martin's bed is empty. I can hear him in the bathroom, peeing and humming. That leaves Milly. I stand by her bed, looking down at her hair spread across the pillow. She's so beautiful at rest, I'm hesitant to touch her. I tap her shoulder lightly, then again, until finally she opens her eyes and gazes up at me.

"Good morning, Milly." As my voice hits her ears, her eyes

blink and narrow, and she rolls over to face the wall, to will herself back to the dream world she forged in the night, where her life is different and better, where more suitable people stand over her. I should tap her again, lift her shade, give her the razzle-dazzle rise-and-shine "Hello world!" routine my dad used to do for us, but instead I back out of the room, ruing my accent and wishing I had saved more before leaving the United States so I didn't have to be here, making this girl homesick in her own home.

"Okay," John says to me back in the kitchen, before I can tell him that Milly isn't getting up, "they both need a thermos with cordial; orange does fine—it comes back half full either way. I give them two snacks, crackers and Vegemite, right, then a sandwich." He picks up a pair of Milly's sunglasses. "Put these in her pack. Not sure she ever wears them, but—" He sounds resigned to the general nonchalance of his children. I wonder if all parents are, or if this is specific to John. "Kids! Let's go! Breakfast!" He never stops moving, tracking the time like a basketball player watches the shot clock.

"Should I get some cereal going?" I ask, wanting to be useful.

"No. Toast. They like toast. I got it." He cuts two slices of bread off a brown loaf.

When I was growing up, my mom would have loved to call toast breakfast. She doesn't go in for *whole big productions*. It just makes a mess, and *Guess who cleans it up?* But my dad, oblivious or determined—I could not say which—preferred a dinerlike experience. He manned the cooktop in his pajamas and a bathrobe, making eggs, any kind you liked, including poached, which required a different pan and special vinegar. He'd fry a pound of bacon, creating a Lincoln Log arrangement on the paper towels, and on special days he added something called scrapple to the menu, a morning meat treat famous throughout the Philadelphia area, notorious elsewhere, involving internal organs and entrails.

In addition to the *holy mess of it all,* my mother opposed the grand breakfast on moral grounds. She was trying to raise kids who ate whatever was put in front of them, then here comes Mr. Wonderful with his magic spatula, taking orders. *Sunnyside up, one in the hole, over easy? Coming right up, Lovey!* He spoiled my mother's carefully calibrated economy, like the well-meaning tourist paying twenty dollars for a basket the locals would trade for a cigarette.

Of John's expedient breakfast, my mom would say *Damn right.*

"Okay, now——" He sets two hats on the counter that look like the straw skimmers people used to wear at Eisenhower rallies. "They must wear caps, it's a rule, part of the uniform. And you should also wear one whenever you're outside. The sun is terribly strong here." Many Australians have told me this, and they all sound the same, like an apologetic host warning guests about the steep driveway.

Just then Milly wanders in, at a tenth of her father's pace, and leans into his side, squinting at me like I'm a headwind. Martin's behind her in nothing but his underwear. I guess everybody's family when you're five.

"Morning, Keely," he says, waving around his silver plastic sword and audacious joie de vivre.

"Morning," I say, mirroring his easy tone, pretending it isn't ludicrous to be standing smack in the middle of their lives, my conspicuousness so acute I can barely look Milly in the eye.

After breakfast and a burst of last-minute activity—sash! library book! pencil case!—the kids are in the car.

"Keely, will you help do my seat belt?" Martin asks.

"Absolutely."

"I like it tight. Do it really tight."

"Yes, sir. And here, this is Blistex, for all that chapping." He purses his lips for me, and I coat them good.

"Keely, my bag is stuck," he says. I shimmy it out. And then, "Keely, can you do my shoe?" I love him for needing me.

"Martin, you can tie your own shoe!" John snaps. I step back, and after a moment John follows up with "Are we all set?" in a different tone—contrite, with a red bow of mustered cheer.

With everyone finally belted in, John backs out the driveway, past a thick hedge that covers Pop's window.

"Bye, Pop!" Martin cries out.

"He can't hear you," Milly snarls.

"Yes, he can!"

"No, he can't . . ." She trails off, bored. Even making sure Martin knows how dumb he is, how inferior and juvenile, doesn't feel as good as having me here feels bad.

Just inside the gates of Wallaby Elementary, Martin stops to stare at a large hole in the ground. "Where went the tree?" he asks.

"I guess they took it out," John says as he nods to a few moms, who send back sorry smiles. He's the only dad on campus.

"It's gone?" Martin asks, gaping at the dirt. "All the way gone?"

"Yup," John says.

"Why?" Martin wants to know.

"I don't know, might have had root rot," John says as he picks up the pace, his hand on Martin's back to keep him moving along. "Sometimes trees get diseased."

Milly stops abruptly, her mouth falling open a little, until

John turns around and taps his watch. "Hey, hey, hurry up," he calls to her. She's looking over at the hole in the ground. "The bell's about to ring."

We push through the swarm of children. As we get to the center of the hive, a giant buzzing of a hundred high-pitched voices bounces off the classrooms. Martin pairs off with someone's little brother. Milly is met by two friends.

"Emma 1 and Emma 2," John explains.

We cross the courtyard, sidestepping balls, so I can shake hands with Milly's teacher, who is waiting to greet his students.

"Mr. Graham, this is our nanny, Kelly. She'll be dropping off and picking up whenever I'm out of town for work." Mr. Graham is young and tan and looks like he swam in the Pacific before school. If my mom saw Mr. Graham, she'd poke me and say, *Get the net.* (My mom started talking like this after her elbow surgery. She got it from her physical therapist, a bulky gal my mom said was *a kill* who told her to *stay cool* and *cut me a break* and *suck it up.*)

"Great to meet you," Mr. Graham says.

"Thanks, you too," I say, wishing I'd worn different clothes, maybe my yellow overall shorts, the ones that scream *Cartwheels! Lemonade! Good times!*

John hangs Milly's bag on her assigned hook while I work to endear myself to Person of Interest #2, Mr. Graham. "The States, yeah . . . Philadelphia, about two hours south of New York." I've found that in the absence of the usual shorthand we use at home—where you went to school, who your mom and dad are—people need to place you physically to start to understand you.

Mr. Graham could definitely be my Australian boyfriend. We could flirt at drop-off and pickup; I could volunteer to help out with papier-mâché or give a talk to the class about America the Beautiful; we could make eyes in the art room, brush up against each other in the supply closet; until finally he stops me behind the PE shed, unclips my sunny overalls, watches them fall to the ground, lifts me up and out of them, at which point I give in, wrapping my bare, tan, definitely shaved legs around his waist like the scene from *Ghost*. Talk about things happening when you leave the house.

In the middle of my *full-court press,* as my mother would put it, a wail goes up from across the playground, and all heads turn. Milly is in a heap under the monkey bars. Emma 1 and Emma 2 squat beside her, giving her the *There, there* treatment. John runs to pick her up, and Martin pats her hair while she bleats like a lamb. I grab her water bottle and jog over, even though I'm probably making a fool out of myself with my amateur gesture.

"Do you want some?" I say in a hypersensitive voice. Milly doesn't look at me but John gives me a nod of thanks. I stand by quietly, along with Martin, Emma 1, and Emma 2, mad at myself for attending to the wrong things.

The buzzer rings. Kids move from their mothers to their classrooms.

"All better?" John says. Milly shakes her head no and cries fiercely, taking this opportunity to set free some tiny bit of the rage and agony packed up inside her.

Eventually, Emma 2 takes Milly's hand, and they head to class, slowly, hunched together like two grandmothers on a slick sidewalk.

"That was a pretty bad fall," I say.

"She'll be fine," John replies, though he's shaking his head and blushing, like it was his fault that she fell or his fault that it took so long for her to settle down. I'm not sure why, but he's guilty about something. A half step ahead of me, he mutters to himself: "The *tree*. I knew the second I said it . . ." The tree? I don't know what's going on, so I walk quietly next to Martin until John turns around and announces that it's time to go to Martin's school.

"Daddy, I don't have school until afternoon time," he says, scooting behind John and pulling on the bottom of his Team Qantas T-shirt. "Piggyback."

John squats so Martin can climb on. "Right."

"Let's go have some nice good licorice," Martin suggests.

"Sure," John agrees, his stamina shot. He'll follow anyone with a plan, even if that anyone is a five-year-old trolling for sugar. "Careful—" John loosens Martin's hands around his neck. "Remember, I have to breathe."

On the way to the car, John stares ahead while Martin chirps on his back, telling me about all the times he's fallen off the monkey bars—so many times! One story reminds him of the next.

"I'm a cheeky monkey! That's what Mummy says."

His freewheeling reference to her and, more than that, his use of present tense make my stomach clench up. Maybe this explains Martin's buoyancy. Maybe he doesn't yet understand that his mother is gone, all-the-way gone.

After we get home from the market and put away what seems like a small amount of food, Martin bounces off to his room.

"He's a kick," I say to John, who is blank-faced, leaning against the pantry door. We stand there like that for a minute, strangers sensing our strangerness.

Then, sudden as a sneeze, John says, "All right, well, that's that."

"Can I help you with anything else?"

He stops and looks at me like it's been a long time since anyone around here asked him that.

"No-no—"

Rather than turning to leave, John stares past me at a dish towel or a pot, something he hasn't noticed in a while, something that has a story in it. I stand still and stay quiet. Must be a minute now. No, more. Maybe he's having the corollary moment to the one I had that morning when Martin appeared, defenseless in his undies: *Who . . . how . . . why is this person standing in my kitchen?*

"So, you're good?" I say finally.

"I said *diseased*. At school. At drop-off. That's a bad word." The hairs on my arm rise as he rolls out of the kitchen and down the hall.

He managed another morning. He got his kids up and dressed, fed and brushed, zipped and buckled in. He forced independence, insisted on safety, babied a little, barked a little. There were gross misunderstandings and the careful metering of information and truth and licorice. He quieted Milly, carried Martin, and suppressed every emotional reaction to every reminder of his wife's absence. The tree with root rot, the fall, the grip so tight he couldn't breathe. He did everything right and then he obliterated it all with one word. *Diseased*.

He slips into his room and closes the door. Before I can make a decision about where to go, I hear John sit on his bed, sigh, fall back, and then, after the springs settle, cough out a muffled cry that might be the worst sound I've ever heard.

Day two is quiet. Just me and Martin.

John's gone to a half-day safety seminar at Qantas, and Milly's down at the park with Emma 1 and her mom. Pop's door is closed, and Evan, the stepson, has yet to surface. I can't believe John didn't feel obliged to involve either one of them in the interview process, at least *a sniff test*, as my mother would call it. And now that I'm here, are they not remotely curious that someone new has moved in? You wouldn't be in my house for three minutes before I'd want to size you up.

"You need anything?" I ask Martin as I shake his pillow back into its case.

"No," he says without looking up from his LEGO men in race cars. "Faster! Faster!"

I fold his camo blanket and pick up around him—socks, playing cards, an apple core, a couple of glasses on the windowsill. The room instantly looks better, cared for.

In the kitchen, I run a damp rag over the counters and close the drawers and put a pencil back in a cup jammed with pens, crayons, and markers. My eyes dart around the room. What else should I do?

On slow babysitting gigs in high school, I was what you'd call a classic snooper. One long night at Mrs. Battel's, I went through her whole makeup bag, trying on all her lipsticks, then moving on to eyeliners and shadows. At the Perrys', I discovered a stack of *Playboys* under the bathroom sink that made my hands sweat, along with an eye-popping hardback book featuring pencil sketches of people having sex in every conceivable position and location, including on a motorcycle. In my own house, when my parents went out, I opened all the drawers and cabinets in their bedroom, flipping through boxes of canceled checks, appointment books, manila envelopes marked *Buick Roadmaster* and *Basement Leak,* eager to place my family on some continuum. Were we broke? Did my parents have sexy secrets?

In my mother's bottom desk drawer, I found two flip sleeves of three-by-three photos with dates stamped in the white margin, mostly of my brothers and me when we were cute—no hair in our eyes or big clipboard teeth coming in at off angles. The second sleeve was more of my mom and her friends, who anointed themselves the Pigeons in the early seventies, a self-effacing downgrade from the Hens. In one picture, my mom and her pal were wearing rented black-and-white maid uniforms and had pots upside down on their heads. They were laughing so hard my mom's face was bright red, and tears ran down her cheeks. Her friend was crossing her legs like she might pee right there in the living room. What were they doing? *Oh God, I couldn't begin to tell you,* my mom said when I asked. I looked at the photo so many times. I'd never seen the madcap woman my mother appeared to be in that photograph.

There was a copy, unopened, of *I'm OK, You're OK* on her nightstand. The back cover posed two questions in all caps: ARE YOU FEELING OK ABOUT YOURSELF? OR STILL PLAYING DESTRUCTIVE GAMES? I remember cracking the spine and flipping through the pages. I liked the idea that all interactions could be described in one of four ways. Most people, the author said, are trapped in *I'm not OK; you're OK* from age three on. My mom would definitely say she was OK. She did not play interpersonal games, destructive or otherwise. My guess was that the book was foisted on her by a freshly converted evangelist for transactional analysis, and she tucked it in her purse, knowing she'd never read it. But then, it was on her nightstand . . .

There was also a hardback copy of *Your Erogenous Zone*—or *The Erogenous Zone* or *Her Erogenous Zone*—something about bodily hot spots, which implied that my parents had sex, and with the intention to please. But we won't be going into any of that, as that is *nobody's damn business*.

I had no sense of what my mom did when she wasn't standing in front of me. I don't know how fulfilled she was or wasn't, whether the designs she had for her life were coming along nicely or growing more laughable every day. I'm not sure she even had designs for her life. But I can tell you this: If my mom wrote a book, it would not be about feeling OK or perfecting the sex act. *Certainly not!* My mom's book would be called: *Work Hard, Save Your Money, Go to Church*.

On the Tanners' shelves are books on camping and New South Wales hiking trails and lots of how-to titles. In a row of hardback novels, I see the spine of *My Ántonia* by Willa Cather, one of the few books I know my mother thinks highly of (along with anything by F. Scott Fitzgerald and the New Testament, which she gave me as a Christmas gift the year I specifically asked for magenta moon boots). Blame the distance, but for the first time, I'm curious to know what kind of book my mom thinks is *absolutely marvelous*. I take it down.

In a drawer, I find a shot of Milly as a toddler, holding her baby brother "in hospital," as the Australians say. The image is shadowy, and the paper is covered with fingerprints, big and small, like scuff marks on the floor of a dance studio.

In the next photo, Milly is wearing a dark green sweatshirt

with a pink satin bow—an actual bow, sewn on, at the base of a
bouquet of roses. You can tell she loves it by her posture. She
does not wear it in the rain or sleep in it. It is her special top, and
it defines her, like my red-and-orange-zigzag poncho in grade
school.

In a third shot, a close-up, Milly is cheek to cheek with John,
and I can see she has his eyes. Her cheeks are full, and her teeth
are tiny and new. She looks happy, unguarded; it's an old photo.

The last picture in the drawer is of Ellen Tanner. I'm sure
of it.

"Hi," I say quietly to the woman in my hands.

She looks about thirty. She's wearing pearls and, from what
little I can see, a plain white dress. Her hair is short, a cute,
unassuming cut. Though there's nothing glamorous about her,
she's not unattractive. She looks sweet. Her head is tilted in
toward a man I assume is her father. He has his arm around her
and is bald, with a comically hooked nose, like a Muppet. Her
eyes are closed—the photographer caught her in a blink—but
their crescent shape reminds me of a girl I knew in college, a
backstabber named Becca who all the boys loved because,
whenever she laughed, her quarter-moon eyes made her look
totally adorable. The association makes me wonder if Martin
and Milly's mother was as lovely and loving as I've made her in
my mind. For all I know, she was manipulative, judgmental,
exacting. Or things less damning but less endearing: gossipy,
edgy, long-winded. You never know after a person dies. There
are no narcissists in eulogies. Nobody raises a glass to Aunt
Joanie, passive-aggressive, at a wake.

But I can tell that she *was* lovely and loving because this is the
picture she kept, the one with her father, the one with her eyes
closed, the one with the lean.

That's it. Four photos. No vacation shots, not climbing a mountain or running in the waves, no record of the big, exciting days, just a random assortment of nothing much.

Rather than settle in front of the television to see how Bonnie Blair and Kristi Yamaguchi did last night in the Olympics, I decide to catch up on my journal in the living room so I can see people coming: John, the stepson, the old man. I put a red blanket over my legs. It's not nearly as warm in Sydney as I expected. Every day starts at sixty degrees, and it takes hours for the sun to fill the house. Leaning over my notebook like I'm ninety, I wonder who knitted this blanket—a grandmother, an auntie, some housebound octogenarian neighbor.

I hear a noise, a window opening, maybe a door.

Do I look too at home? What if Pop walks in and finds a stranger wrapped up in his favorite blanket? What if it was his daughter's? What if this was her spot, the place she rested after surgery or chemotherapy, under her best wool blanket?

Impossible. No one would leave a reminder of that magnitude lying around where any ignorant visitor might casually put it into rotation. Someone thoughtful would have boxed up all the emblems of her illness.

Just in case, I stand and fold the blanket and slip back into my room.

I hate this.

I've just about made it through my first week. Tomorrow is Friday.

After the kids head to school with John and I've washed all the breakfast dishes, I settle into one of the four boxy gold velvet chairs in front of the TV to start reading *My Ántonia*. The wide flat arms of the chairs are dotted with marker. The welting is colored in by hand. *Scribbling on furniture,* I hear my mother say. *What's next? Painting the carpet?*

Though maybe the free-for-all started after the mother got sick. I bet you'd do that. I bet you'd stop saying no all the time so that, later, if your kids were thinking about you, they'd remember you smiling, thumbs up, being the Fun Mom, the Best Mom, the mom with the singsong voice who says, *Go ahead, sweetie! That's great, honey!*

I would. If I got sick, I'd say yes to every last thing until the day I died. Hot dogs for breakfast, bubble gum in school, sleepovers on weeknights. No more teeth brushing or bed making. Turn up the music, break out the pottery wheel, pass the markers. Indelible? PERFECT. I'd hang up all their drawings and photos and certificates and ribbons until the walls were covered from floor to ceiling. I'd surround myself with evidence of life, proof that my kids were waxing even as I waned.

I'm only a page in when a guy who looks about twenty-one comes through the sliding glass door in shorts and nothing else.

"Hi, I'm Evan," he says. "The stepson."

"Oh, hi, I'm Kelly," I reply, keeping my eyes from drifting over his bare chest.

I close my notebook and we shake hands, which feels courtly and silly, considering his near-nakedness. We're right around the same height—five-seven, five-eight. He has long, loose hair that falls just past his shoulders; it's brown, but you can tell he was blond as a child. He's taut and muscular, vacuum-packed, like the soccer players I knew in high school. He has perfect teeth, and dimples. Dimples kill me.

"Uh, excuse me." He disappears down the hall and comes back wearing a T-shirt. My eyes relax.

"I was gonna stir up some eggs," he says, pulling his hair into a ponytail. "You like eggs?"

"Oh, thanks, no, I'm good." Why am I nervous?

In a minute, he's back, sitting behind me at the kitchen table with a pile of eggs that nearly covers the plate. "Mind if I turn on the TV?" he says.

"Not at all."

He clicks through the stations and stops on a laundry detergent commercial. "Does that say Channel Ten?" he asks, squinting.

"Where? Oh, yeah, Ten."

"Ever watch Santa Barbara?" Evan asks.

"No. I don't think so."

"It's from America. They live in California," he explains, in case inference was beyond me.

On the screen comes a blonde named Eden, who, I quickly surmise, has been raped. Her husband, Cruz, a bulky Mexican guy, kneels beside her, running the backs of his fingers along her cheek as she weeps, tending to her perfectly, like people do on TV.

I've never known a guy who watches soap operas.

At a commercial, Evan ferries his plate into the kitchen and comes back with the newspaper and a pencil.

"U.S. Great Lake, four letters," Evan says, sitting down, leaving an empty chair between us. I've never known a guy who does the crossword.

"Uh, HOMES: Huron, Ontario, Michigan, Erie."

"Yep. There she is."

Evan checks off the clue with a *tcht* of satisfaction and pulls a bag of sunflower seeds out of his pocket.

I try him on in my mind. Me and Evan, Evan and me. It could work. I could see it. He's young, but what's a couple of years at this point? We could bump into each other over dishes, yard work, laundry. We could have a beer one night, wait for John to go to his room, make out in front of the TV, sneak back to wherever Evan sleeps, get horizontal, roll around for a while, spoon, do it all over again the next day.

I know, I do this with everyone (well, not John), but someday one of the people I mentally audition will become my actual boyfriend and then my fiancé and then my husband and it will have started just like this. Hi. *Hi*. I'm Kelly. *I'm* _____.

"John went to get paint," I tell Evan.

"Pfft," he says in a way that begs interpretation. Unimpressed? Dismissive? Whatever it is, I am not inclined to mention John again.

Evan asks about my travels, so I launch into *Things happen when you leave the house* and then fast-forward to selling Tracy on the trip, arriving in Sydney, hitting all the bars and restaurants, getting hired and fired by human-rights violator Eugenia Brown, seeing John's ad, and Tracy's gig in Beecroft.

"It's weird to go so many days in a row without seeing her. We were together so much in college, people called us Trelly."

Just then, Pop shuffles out of his room. He is, as photographed, almost entirely bald, with a nose that draws a second look. His skin is pink, and his eyes, small and set back, are Paul Newman blue.

"Well, hello," he says, looking down at the two of us in front of what my mom calls *the idiot box*.

I stand to shake his hand, which is cool and smooth, like a river stone. "Hi, I'm Kelly."

"Yes, I see. You can call me Pop. Evan," he addresses his grandson, "how was your trip? You back at work tonight?" It turns out Evan was camping the past few days and has a job stocking shelves at a grocery warehouse from eleven P.M. to five A.M., which explains why he's so muscular, not that I'm fixated on his body or anything, but, I mean, he is very fit.

"Can I make you some coffee?" I ask Pop.

"No, thank you, I'm out here to get the laundry going," he says, patting the last of his hair absently.

"I can do that—"

"Pop does the washing," Evan cuts me off, sounding almost paternal.

Pop makes his way slowly down the hall toward the kids' room, making an airy whistling sound. When I ask Evan if I should gather all the dirty clothes, he assures me that Pop doesn't need any help.

So now I've met all of Ellen Tanner's people. The newish husband. The young children, the nearly grown son, the father. If this family were a poker hand, you'd fold. Without that middle card, you're drawing to an inside straight, and that almost never works out.

It isn't long before John pulls in the driveway. I hear him at

the front door. I'm not eager to be found sitting in front of the
TV with Evan while an old man does the washing. I walk to the
hall to see if I can help carry anything, but when John gets inside, he nods at me, steps into his room, and shuts the door, just
like yesterday.

Back in the TV area, Evan's seat is empty, the newspaper
gone, Pop is back in his space, and I'm alone in a house where
one seven-year-old girl and three grown men sequester themselves voluntarily. I itch for Martin, easy Martin, who needs me
to listen to his piano piece and buckle his seat belt. If no one will
take my help, at least give me some pool tiles to scrub.

I suppose my job here could be to help John see his children
as irresistible rascals again before he starts to resent their youth
and ignorance and untimely needs. Maybe the great service
I can offer John is to take over the crap parts, the stuff my
mom did—*No no no* and *Eat your beans* and *Stop that right this
minute*—so he can be a beaming dad who tickles and brings
home presents from gift shops and says, *Come here, Lovey! Give
your old man a hug.*

Tracy's here to meet everyone.

"You must be Martin," she says, bending down with her hand out.

"Of course I am," he says. "What's your name?"

"Tracy Tuttle."

"What's your mum's name?" Tracy looks stricken, but I give her a *don't worry, he does this* smile. To him, there's nothing sad or heavy about it; it's an old rubber band that he shoots at people for fun.

"Michele."

"And this is Milly," I insert before Martin can reload.

"Hello, Milly."

"Hi," she says, dead to Tracy's warmth, as she falls back on the couch like a thirteen-year-old whose mother just suggested, say, *a nice pair of denim gauchos* for the school dance. Though, of course, she never will be.

While Martin pulls Tracy into his room to meet his cast of dinosaurs, I walk around the back, looking for John, who is sanding the window trim.

"Hi Jo—"

He spins around. Even though he put the ad in the *Herald* and interviewed me and prepared the guest room for my arrival, I am still a constant surprise.

"Oh, sorry, hello," he says, blinking at me.

"I didn't mean to startle you. My friend Tracy's here, and we're headed into the city, but I wanted to introduce you and ask if she could spend the night in my room, maybe."

"Of course, right, good."

Tracy finds us out back. She and John shake hands and she compliments the new paint color. He says thanks, like he knows she's just making conversation because that's his whole life now.

On the way out, we pass Evan in the driveway. I introduce Tracy, but we can't hang around and talk because we're catching the 5:18 to Kings Cross.

On the way to the pub, we stop in a pharmacy to primp. Terra-cotta bronzing powder, purple eye shadow, a spritz of Calvin Klein Eternity. Once we're properly *tarted up,* as my mother says, we walk faster, the sad, screwy life of the Tanners falling off me with every step. We pass three tattoo parlors, a leather store, and a record shop spraying punk music onto the street. A bohemian at the bus stop is reading Sartre. Now *this* is what I left home for.

At the Den, we settle in with two pints of Victoria Bitter to hear a singer-songwriter we saw advertised on a flyer in the train station bathroom last week. Tracy takes out our box of Parliaments, a jumbo pack with an incredible *fifty* cigarettes. Smoking is idiotic, I know. I've seen the pictures of dirty lungs, but I'm young, and we don't have cancer in our family. Anyway, I'll quit before I have kids.

It's a relief, being at the pub with Tracy. The Australian code of conduct—backslapping, high-fiving, nicknaming—is pure Corrigan. The louder, the better. The only time I feel like I'm in a new country altogether is in the Tanner house.

Before we finish our first pint, we get talking with some Irish guys who ask what we're doing in Sydney. We tell them about *our kids*. When I explain the Tanner situation, the one guy says, "God, my house woulda gone straight to pieces. My ma did everythun."

"While your da and my da were down the pub," the other says, laughing. "I'll tell ya this straight: I don' think there's a fader in our whole village coulda raised his own kids. Most of 'em were a sorry fookin' mess half the time."

"My dad didn't go to bars, but he didn't do much of the dirty work, either," I say, stopping to look at the truth of that for the first time. He blew in at the end of each day, fresh from the club—steamed, showered, and doused in Clubman aftershave—after a game of tennis or squash on the way home, looking for two boys to roughhouse and one girl to hug and squeeze until she laughed and said *Daaad*. That schedule left all unpleasant tasks to my mom, who liked to point out, *Your father's the glitter but I'm the glue*. I never knew how their roles were distributed, whether they fell out naturally from the get-go or they evolved over time, one creating the other through negotiations and tiny adjustments along the way. I suppose early on she got a sense of what Greenie could handle, and what she could tolerate not being done her way, and compensated accordingly.

However it emerged, my mother was the lead on matters requiring adult intervention, and as such she came to have a high tolerance for crisis, something I learned the fall of my sophomore year when, one afternoon for no good reason, I skipped field hockey practice to go shoplifting at Sears with my friend Louise.

I only signed up for field hockey because my dad got a kick out of me playing sports, and on game days I got to wear the team uniform, which involved a very short kilt that my mother could not ban me from leaving the house in. Other than flashing my bloomers, I hated it—the running and crouching and whacking—and was terrible at all of it.

That Friday, Louise and I looked at each other as we headed to the locker room and decided to keep walking, past the showers, out through the smoking section, up the back hill, along the baseball field, across the street, through the giant double doors into Sears, where apparel spread out before us like a field of cornstalks. We ran our hands along the shirts and sweaters, making snobbish noises to signal our superiority to these garments and the people who bought them. We went down to the basement, past the portrait studio, to the candy counter. I took a pack of gum and slid it into my pants pocket. Just because. For kicks, Louise lifted a roll of Spree and slipped it into her oversize acid-washed jean jacket.

We went back to Jewelry. Long gold chains hung in clusters by length. We tried on three or four of them, moving away from the counter to see ourselves in the full-length mirrors, making sure, I guess, that the necklaces worked with our widewales and Docksiders. I unclasped one of the hooks and dropped a chain into my book bag. I could hear my new necklace slide down my world history textbook, along the cover I made from a brown Acme bag because Momma Pennywise didn't believe in buying glossy Go-Go's textbook covers from the school supplies store.

Next, we went to Hosiery, pulsing with anarchy. I saw my mom's standard panty hose hanging on a rack. Suntan, control top, reinforced toe. Her birthday was in a week. I took five pairs. I could picture her face as she opened them. She wouldn't be happy I'd spent so much money on her, but she would love the practicality of the gift. Everyone needs a good supply of hose.

We crossed the aisle into Accessories. I hung a denim purse over my shoulder and walked back and forth, modeling for Louise. She said it was super cute and a good size. I pulled out the paper wadded up inside and stuffed it in a rounder of dungarees. I folded the purse in half and pushed it deep into my book bag. It was so easy, we were laughing.

"Holy shit!" we whispered to each other on the way to the exit. "What a joke."

We passed through the first set of doors, ready to scream with relief. As we pushed against the rail that opened the second set of doors and the air of freedom hit us, a man took both of us by our elbows and said, "Okay, girls, you can come with me," and I wanted to fall over so he couldn't take me to wherever he was leading us.

I hated myself.

I hated both of us.

The man guided us through racks of winter coats until we got to a door with no trim, no doorknob, and no sign. He unlocked it with the smallest key on his giant ring and sat us down in an office. "Empty your bags."

We poured everything onto his desk. He patted down our bags and opened zipped compartments, even the pocket where Louise kept tampons. He didn't care that we were crying. He made a list of everything we'd stolen and tallied up the value. My pile was worth almost fifty dollars.

He asked how old we were, and when we said fifteen, he shook his head and pushed clipboards toward us. "Write down your name, address, and telephone number."

I watched him dial Wooded Lane. It was so awful to listen to his deep, imperial voice telling my mother her daughter had been shoplifting and was "in his custody" that I sobbed. My nose was running, but the man didn't offer me a Kleenex, or push the box on the desk closer to me. I didn't deserve a tissue. I wiped the snot on my sleeve.

Louise's mom, whom I loved, came first. She glared at both of us and said she was *disgusted*. She did not like me anymore, I could tell. She would never again say, "Hey, Lou Lou, why don't you see if Kelly can come up to the lake with us this summer?"

They left, and I was alone with the security officer.

It was getting dark outside. Must've been thirty minutes since Lou's mom came. When my mother finally arrived, she did not look at me. She shook the officer's hand and said, "I wouldn't have blamed you if you called the police and sent her to jail."

"I'm sorry," I whispered.

She said nothing.

We walked through the parking lot to the station wagon. She unlocked her door and got in. After sitting alone in the car for a moment, she slowly leaned over to pull up the lock on my side. I slid in and pulled the door closed. My mom put the keys in the ignition and then fell back in her seat.

"Mm," she said without starting the car. "Mm-mm."

"I took the panty hose for you—"

Her hand flew across the space between us and she slapped me across the face. I cried, turning toward the window to look at the empty black parking lot, and on the glass there was a little splatter of blood. I touched my nose. It was bleeding. "I'm sorry," I cried. "I'm so sorry."

"Mm-mm," she said again, shaking her head, her lips tight.

At last she turned on the car. "I'm not going tell your father one word about this. I don't think he could handle it. Honest to God, I don't."

Shoplifting was so bad that she could not tell my dad, my booster and biggest fan. The fall would be too far. It would hurt too much. He would love me less if he knew. Which meant that either she loved me less as of that moment, or her love was different than his. Our relationship started pristine but was pretty beat-up by that point, like an heirloom tablecloth that, after years of hard use, was tired and stained. Maybe she was hoping that didn't have to happen with my dad just yet. Or ever.

Whatever her reasons, my dad was not told about the Sears episode. He could still run around town waving my flag, bragging about his "Lovey," his "superstar" who played lacrosse in the spring and field hockey in the fall. Only my mother knew I hated sports and worse, much much worse, that I was morally defective. Because only she could handle it.

The morning after Kings Cross, Tracy and I are so hungover we keep my room pitch-black all morning, only letting light in when we leave to use the toilet and take some Tylenol. I'd give up a month of my life for two Alka-Seltzer.

Around one, I pull myself out of bed and stretch, feeling like I'm fifty years old. I can hear John out back, sanding. Evan and Pop are wherever Evan and Pop usually are. Tracy's in the TV room, reading about the election back home. Apparently, the governor of Arkansas just won a primary, but nobody takes him seriously. I mean, he's from Arkansas.

Things are churning and spoiling inside me and my head aches for hydration. Milly, who seems able to see my hangover, is jamming *Beauty and the Beast* into the video player.

"Need some help?" I ask, wincing at the sounds.

"No."

She turns to make sure I'm looking when the tape is sucked into the plastic mouth of the machine. Not for the first time, Milly reminds me of my mom, who likes to do things the way she does them, often ass-backwards. *Oh, wait till you get old,* my mother warns when I start to *interfere.* But it's hard to watch someone struggle with a testy machine, a sticky door, a heavy suitcase, much less listen to them cough or cry. People want to help, and the more we've seen and heard and done, the more useful we are, and this is why even the tiniest show of stoicism, in little girls and grown women, makes me mad. It makes us useless to each other.

Martin pops up and pats the cushion. "Sit here, Keely."

The seat is warm. Martin climbs into my lap with the dingy blanket that he loves and a lumpy pillow that he knuckles the corners of. I don't remember ever watching a movie in my mom's lap. Snuggling is not her speed, and *Tell me, who has time to sit?* Personally, I can think of nothing better, nothing more curative, than tangling up with a kid.

Milly settles into her seat while Tracy brews a pot of coffee in the kitchen. "You all right in there, Kel?"

"My head—"

"Are you sick?" Martin asks.

Milly turns to look at me.

I stop myself from saying what I've said about a hundred hangovers before—my head is killing me.

As the movie begins, Martin turns around and kisses me on the lips.

"Oh!" I say, overcome.

Milly rolls her eyes. I see her point. I can't imagine, now or as a kid, kissing any woman other than my mother, especially on the lips: now because it seems the exclusive right of the woman who raised you, then because it would have been gross.

I send off a silent apology to Ellen Tanner. Though I suppose if she can see us, it's possible that she doesn't mind. In fact, maybe she's euphoric, crying with relief that her son isn't hiding under his bed in the fetal position waiting for her—only her—to coax him back out into the world. Maybe Milly's resistance is what undoes her.

Tracy and I are happily staying in tonight with the kids because John has "plans," unspecified, as usual. Maybe, if Ev hears John's car pull away, he'll come in.

Milly and Martin are on the floor, gluing ripped bits of paper into horses, pigs, and flowers.

"Pretty rose, Milly," I say.

"It's a tree," she says.

"See!" Martin points to the anorexic trunk.

"Oh, right, duh." I comb through Martin's hair with my fingers. "Hey, big news: We're making grilled peanut butter and jelly sandwiches for dinner."

"What are that?"

I explain that they are PB&Js, just grilled.

"P P and J?"

I lead the kids into the kitchen, and Tracy and I describe each step as if we're hosting a cooking segment on morning television.

Now, Kelly, tell me what you have here.

Well, Tracy, we start with a nice thick pat of butter, maybe two, like so . . .

I press the sandwich down with a spatula like a short-order cook, and the peanut butter oozes from the sides. A masterpiece. I wish Evan were here.

I slide the sandwich onto a cutting board and quarter it.

"Keely, Tracy Tuttle!" Martin says after his first bite. "This—this is magnificent!"

Milly will not join Martin's chorus, but she finishes every bite and accidentally lets out an *mmm* that I pretend not to relish.

Night comes and turns the sliding glass doors into blocks of glossy black. I go back to the kids' room to deliver the bad news: bedtime. Martin folds easily enough. Milly looks mutinous but pushing back would require engagement. As my mother liked to remind me after going fifteen rounds over mascara or red fingernail polish, *You have to care to fight.*

"Night, Keely," Martin calls out. "Good night, Tracy Tuttle!"

I squeeze his foot through his blanket and flip on Milly's daisy night-light. I'm getting the hang of them.

Tracy and I stay up late playing Rummy 500 on the kitchen table and whispering about the kids. Tracy goes over on three aces, which means she gets the bed and I'm on the floor. I settle in with my Walkman, listening to a George Winston tape from college, staring at the skylight, which is framing the moon like a piece of art. This is as good as I have felt in this house. I flip through the headlines of my day, looking for the source—no Evan, no outings, barely a breath of fresh air—until I get there: *Milly said "mmm."* I made Milly Tanner a tiny bit happy.

The next day, Milly opens the mailbox and pulls out a stack of junk mail, much of which is addressed to Ellen Tanner. I wonder what it feels like to see her mother's name so often, though it's clear to me now that you hardly need a pile of catalogs to keep your mother on your mind.

"Anything good?" I ask, sitting on the stoop, watching her spread out the mail on the porch.

She holds up a letter from the U.S. "Look! It's from your mum! Open it!" Milly says, presenting the envelope to me as if it's a FedEx from an enchanted forest.

"I will," I say, underplaying it as best I can. I can see how curious she is.

"Now!" She hovers by my shoulder. I can smell her primal jealousy. I hand her a catalog and tell her to pick out a top she likes, but she won't be distracted. "Read it!" Her interest in my mother elevates my own, like when you see someone staring into the distance and you automatically turn to see the object of their attention.

"All right, but find a cool outfit," I say, tapping the catalog.

The letter's nothing special. They watched *Crocodile Dundee* in my honor. They think Paul Hogan is Mel Gibson. My dad backed over the mailbox with the car again. Why won't he use the rearview mirror? The orange daylilies by the driveway have bloomed. I shake my head as I read.

"What?" She wants to know what's making me grin.

"My mom is telling me about her flowers."

Toward the end, my mom discloses that she's concerned about John, like maybe he's going to sneak into my room at night and force himself on me. *John!* Some prig at the club probably made a crack about Joey Buttafuoco, and now my mom's up at night, picking off her fingernail polish. The letter ends with my mom's *strong suggestion* that I lock my door at night.

"What?" Milly asks, dying to know what made my expression darken.

"You know, sometimes, my mother is just—" I don't know how to end the sentence. I don't know what I can tell her.

"What?" She wants to daughter vicariously.

"I don't know what she's talking about. She doesn't always make sense."

The thing about mothers, I want to say, is that once the containment ends and one becomes two, you don't always fit together so neatly. They don't get you like you want them to, like you think they should, they could, if only they would pay closer attention. They agonize over all the wrong things, cycling through one inane idea after another: seat belts, flossing, the Golden Rule. The living mother-daughter relationship, you learn over and over again, is a constant choice between adaptation and acceptance.

The only mothers who never embarrass, harass, dismiss, discount, deceive, distort, neglect, baffle, appall, inhibit, incite, insult, or age poorly are dead mothers, perfectly contained in photographs, pressed into two dimensions like a golden autumn leaf. That's your consolation prize, Milly Tanner. Your mother will never be caught sunbathing in the driveway in her bra or cheapened by too much drink. She'll never be overheard bitching to the phone company or seen slamming her bedroom door in fury. Your mother will always be perfect.

But who would say such things to a girl so electric with envy?

John has loads to review with me before he leaves town. Outgoing mail, including a bill that has to be paid but not until tomorrow, a note for Mr. Graham that I'm eager to deliver. Emergency contacts. Pizza money. Directions. Martin needs this, Milly likes that, check on Pop if you haven't seen him by eleven A.M., Evan doesn't need anything, John explains, like a zookeeper handing out care-and-feeding instructions for all the animals, the ones he's cared for since birth and the ones that came with the park.

He looks commanding in his pressed Qantas blues, more like a pilot than a flight attendant. I bet this is what he was wearing the day he met Ellen. Maybe they crossed paths in the Sydney airport, waiting for a morning flight—John self-assured among his colleagues, talking twin engines and load factors; Ellen impressed by his manly knowledge. Playing the wingman, his workmate asks Ellen where she lives . . . does she travel often . . . with her husband? When she says she's divorced, John steps in, buys her a cup of tea, a cranberry scone. His crew is summoned over the PA but John hangs back, asks if he can ring her sometime. She blushes while she writes out her phone number on a paper coaster. She watches him walk away, wondering if he might be someone important to her someday, someone to have and hold until death do them part.

"Remember," John says to me, "the next-door neighbor's number is on the pad in the kitchen if you need anything."

"Yeah, and I have Evan." He raises his eyebrows like I'm counting on the town drunk. Never mind that I've been taking showers and blow-drying my hair every morning for that bum.

"I've left some money on the counter for pizza or groceries."

"Yup. Thanks."

After John leaves, I close the front door and head back to the living room with my book. I have three hours until I pick up the kids.

My Ántonia is set in Nebraska around the time that train travel was taking off. It's one giant flashback, narrated by Jim, a grown man recalling his memories of a hardworking bohemian girl he knew when he was young. We learn in the prologue that they lost touch when he went east for college, but she never left his mind. He thinks of her often, probably more than a married man should, and when he does, she's bathed in sunlight, running across a prairie in a homemade sundress. It's all very romantic and nostalgic, and I love it straight off. But my mother? She doesn't go for *a lot of golden-light nonsense*.

Or so I thought. What do I know?

I know that my mother loves sauerkraut and anchovies and pearl onions. I know she prefers mashed potatoes from a box, and when she wants to, she can peel an orange in one go. I know she likes her first drink to be vodka—one full jigger, over ice, with a lemon rind—and then she downgrades to Chardonnay, which she pours into the same glass over the same ice with the same piece of lemon floating on top, *one less dish to wash*. I know her favorite movie is either *Gone with the Wind* or *Pretty Woman,* whichever comes to mind first. She considers house pets and clothes you can't wash in a machine and changing lip colors with the seasons *ridiculous*. I know she doesn't think fathers need to know every single thing about their children. She feels her best on her knees after Communion and thinks too many people treat church like a fashion show or a social outing, and she has no words for the Christmas and Easter Catholics except *That's between them and the good Lord above*. I know she has an old silver rosary under her pillow, where she can find it in the night when she starts fretting about something that wouldn't have a chance against her in the light of day, and next to her rosary is her *huffa-puffa,* for her asthma, which gets worse in the summer and when she worries.

Maybe what I don't know is that she secretly lives for a good love story.

Maybe, like my dad says, she's a romantic, something I've always dismissed as biased.

My father first laid eyes on her at a wedding. He told me the story on a car ride to Baltimore.

"She was a bridesmaid for Cousin Nancy. I went over there to pick up my grandmother, and the whole gang, huge bridal party, was out back posing for photos in the yard. You should have seen the camera, Lovey. Big as a suitcase, up on that thing—what do they call it?"

"Tripod?"

"Tripod! Boy, you're quick, Lovey!"

"So, about Mom . . ."

"Best-looking gal in the bunch."

I had seen a photo from that day. My mom's hair was short and swept high off her forehead like Lucille Ball's in one of the serious episodes. Her skin was creamy, and her dress wrapped around her shoulders and hips like it'd been sewn on her that morning.

"How old was she?"

"Young, Lovey. Too young for me!"

"How old were you?"

"Well, let's just say I was a little older than I needed to be at that particular moment. So I did something to make her remember me."

"Like?"

"Oh, a little jig, a soft shoe . . ."

I gave him a look that said if a boy came to our house and did any sort of dance, that'd be the end of him.

"I knew what I was doing, Lovey."

"Keep going."

"During the ceremony, I watched her on the altar, and I could tell she had a BIG-TIME relationship with God."

I knew what he was talking about. On Sundays after communion, during the time set aside for quiet prayer, she'd cover her whole face with her hands, like a girl who knew well her meekness. She'd stay that way, on her knees, longer than all the rest of the congregation, making me wonder what she was telling God, or if she was waiting for Him to speak to her.

"And she's smart."

"How could you tell?"

"You know, that famous Mary Corrigan wit." Everybody's everything was famous, according to my dad.

"Mom?" Most of the time, when she cracked a joke, she had to explain to me that she was *being funny,* and I'm pretty sure that if you have to tell someone you're being funny, you're not.

"Oh, God, yeah! I'd say she was the funniest girl I'd ever met."

"So, did you ask her to dance?"

"Every guy there asked her to dance. But I did a number on

her, Lovey. The Green Man did a number on her. I danced with her mother, too."

"Libby was there?"

"Oh yeah, they all knew each other—my parents, her parents, the whole Catholic mafia."

"Did you talk to TJ?" There was something scary to me about my mom's dad; it could have been his FBI-type glasses or sharp nose or severe jawline. Whatever it was, TJ was not the type to pull pennies from behind your ear. He actually spanked me once. It hurt like hell, and I cried my eyes out, but he didn't care. He thought I was *overindulged*, which was laughable, considering my mother's opposition to everything from baked goods to sleepovers to pierced ears.

"I did what I could to make a positive impression. I may have even suggested I was a few years younger than I actually was. You know, TJ didn't want his little girl running around with some old dog."

"How long before he found out?"

"The next weekend, I asked her to come see my lacrosse game, which she did with a few of her girlfriends, and the Green Man put one in the net for her." I could have guessed this part of the story, or assumed it. Lacrosse often figured in the seminal moments of my family's life. "The next day, the Baltimore *Sun* wrote up the game with a big photo of the Green Man, and underneath, in the little caption part, it said CORRIGAN, AGE 30, SCORES WINNING GOAL."

"Whoops."

He laughed like that was the best reaction anyone could've possibly had to his story. "*Whoops* is right, Lovey! Your mother and your aunt Betsy tried to hide the paper when they saw it, but TJ went straight for the sports section, and *whammo!*, the truth was out." Dancing, fibbing, hiding a paper. There's romance there, I guess.

"You just fell in love right off the bat?"

"She was irresistible," he offers as a matter of fact. After decades of living together, which you would think would dull even the shiniest of starts, my dad's take was stunningly simple: "Angel on my shoulder that day, Lovey."

My mother, a godsend. Hard to imagine.

My dad and I have relived the beats of this story many times since, even though my mom doesn't like him *filling my head with romance*. She thinks his bang-o! version creates unrealistic expectations. *Your father makes it sound like a Gidget movie, Kelly.* Even if she was romantic once, a Baltimore miss who devoured *My Ántonia* and let herself be twirled on a dance floor by a stranger, those girlish days are gone. She was a mother now, my mother, and she didn't trust the dreamy look in my eye, *not one bit*. Picking a husband was a serious matter best done with a cool head.

Well into week two, I learn that Evan has a car, a Volkswagen Scirocco that won't run. I get the feeling he only rolls it out of the garage when John is away. I suppose, without his mother here, it's not Evan's driveway to litter with parts or stain with drops of oil.

"Got the crossword here if you want it," I say, folding back the puzzle page the way he does.

"Any easy ones?"

"Well, three across is *Authority's home*."

"Canberra."

"Oh, right. Two *R*'s?" I ask, even though I know. He nods, the manual open at his feet. Maybe crosswording could be Our Thing. "So, what's wrong with your car?"

"Oh, a lot. But the biggest problem is the transmission."

"You're fixing your own transmission?" I've never known someone who could fix his own transmission.

"I'm trying. I think it's some kind of torque thing." I love the way *torque* sounds coming out of his mouth, part James Bond, part MacGyver. "Anyway, it's worth a try. The shop wants to charge me two hundred and forty quid." *Quid*.

"Wow," I say, wishing I knew something about transmissions, like for instance their function. "So—two across is *Favourite suds show*, which has to be a soap opera, and I thought *Santa Barbara*, but it's only nine letters."

"*Neighbors*." His head is back down under the hood.

"Man, you're good." Transmissions *and* daytime dramas.

"My sister's obsessed with that show."

"I didn't know you had a sister. Other than Milly."

"Yeah, she's at uni. About an hour out."

A hundred questions come to mind, toppling out over one another like beach balls falling from a display tower. *What's your sister's name? Do she and John get along? Why isn't she here helping out?* While we're at it, I'd also like to know how old Evan was when his parents divorced, whether his father remarried, and how far away they live, but before I can ask him anything, he squats down to look closely at the engine diagram, and anyone can read that cue.

"Well, thanks for the *Neighbors* thing. Never would have gotten it."

He looks up. "Okay if I join you all for dinner?"

"Great, I was thinking spaghetti."

I've wondered what Evan does for dinner. I imagined him back in his room, sitting on a milk crate, warming a can of beans on a Bunsen burner. There's something so modest about him. His pastimes and low expectations, the unassuming position he takes with me, the kids, John. He's like a poor kid who belongs to no one, an orphan who doesn't want to make trouble lest he be sent back out on the streets.

My mother would like Evan for his humility and autonomy. Personally, I aim for more conspicuous targets, guys my dad would get a bang out of, guys who tell jokes or have a signature dance move. But there's something about Evan, something that pulls at me. I like him. I know because, just now when he asked to have dinner with us, I calculated how long I'd have to wait to see him again.

Six and a half hours later, Evan shows up in the kitchen with wet hair, wearing a fresh shirt. The kids run to him, crashing into his side.

"You smell like soap!" Martin says.

"I cleaned up for supper. Now, let's help Kelly," he says.

"But we already helped you in your room this afternoon!" Martin reminds Evan.

"Ah, yes! Big help, that's right. Go play, then." The kids peel away. "We cleaned out my camping stuff," he explains to me.

"Fair enough," I say, and hand him a box of pasta. He pours the shells into the boiling water, and I add the last of a bag of macaroni.

"So how easy is it to get to Centennial Park from here?" I float.

"Not hard. You can take the train and then walk."

While I shred carrots onto lettuce that the kids will pick at, Evan grates cheese into a bowl. He moves more freely when John is away, making me wonder why he still lives here. If it's so hard for them to coexist, couldn't Evan move in with his father?

"Going this weekend?" he asks.

"No, next, I think." I could ask him to come, but Tracy says it's better to keep it friendly, *Things could get pretty weird pretty fast,* and I'm sure she's right.

"I'm out of town next weekend," he says. "Not that—"

Pop shuffles by, out of his room at an unusual time.

"You want some noodles?" Evan calls to him.

"Eh?"

Evan holds up the box as a visual aid. "PASTA?"

"No, no, thank you. You go ahead. I'm good." Pop moves on.

"He's something else," I say. "How long has he lived here?"

"A couple years now," Evan says, and I tell him I lived with my grandmother and her bachelor brother for a while. He wants to know about Great-uncle Slug, so I explain that he's tall and bony and wears the same white button-down and blue wool crew-neck sweater every day, even at the height of summer, except Sundays, when he changes to a jacket and tie. He has huge, soft ears sprouting hair and a big nose with cavernous nostrils. He talks, pretty much interchangeably, about his *morning bowel movement,* the Orioles' *damn fine shortstop,* and *the Japs,* who, he is quick to point out, *are going to mop the floor with America.* He's been taking the same woman—May—out to dinner at the same place—Johnny Unitas' Golden Arm—every Thursday night at five P.M. for twenty-seven years. Half the time May pays, and half the time Slugger does, though of course he always drives. He loves his Caddy, identifiable around town by a bumper sticker that would have you believe BALD IS BEAUTIFUL! This is where my mom comes from. These people. How could she not be stingy . . . dogmatic . . . screwy?

"So how's Pop?" I ask.

"Doesn't need much looking after yet."

I guess that's partly why Evan is still here, to watch Pop, who is his blood, not John's.

Dinner is ready. We sit down with the kids, and it feels so close to playing house that I rush us through the meal in about seven minutes.

After dinner, Evan does the dishes, and I watch his shoulders move under his T-shirt. His back is brawny, like the man on the dish-soap label. I have to start exercising. I wonder if they sell Lean Cuisine in Australia.

"I have a brother, too," Evan says as he closes the dishwasher. "Called Andy. He lives with my dad. He used to live here. We all did." Thus come the installments of his family story: sudden and short.

"Older or younger?" I wipe the counter next to him.

"Younger. I'm the oldest." We stay busy when we talk, finding every way not to look at each other.

"I'm the youngest. Two older brothers."

I tell him about GT and Booker. They love sports and parties, they're really funny, they never write. *They'd eat you alive,* I think. They don't do introverts.

"Ev! It's ocean time!" Martin calls from his room.

"What's that?" I ask.

"Martin likes to talk about the oceans."

"Like what?"

"Oh, you know, just all the stats. How deep they are, the temperatures and stuff."

"How deep are they?"

"In the deepest parts, about thirty-two thousand feet."

"Wow."

"And eighty-two percent of the ocean is abyssal in depth." I don't know that word, *abyssal.* It seems right that I should learn it here.

"Ev!" Martin calls again.

"I've got this," I say.

"Ta. And thanks for dinner."

Off he goes, on command, to talk with Martin about the deepest, coldest, darkest parts of the ocean. Which is another reason he's still here.

After two weeks, Evan and I are in a solid routine. It starts with *Santa Barbara*. I take some pride that the show's stylists—who, we were alerted today, won the Daytime Emmy for Outstanding Achievement for Hairstyling—do Eden's hair like I do mine: a good solid hit of spray on the hair over the ears to keep it high off the cheeks, another blast to elevate the bangs. The rest is loose and natural. (Some part of your hair needs to move when you walk, or you look like an ass.)

"I reckon that's it," Evan says as today's episode wraps. "Hey, you haven't seen any hiking boots around here, have you?"

"No, sorry. John gets home in a couple hours—"

"John won't know. I'm not John's . . . problem."

"Maybe Pop?"

On cue, Pop appears. "Look by the back door," he says, handing Evan a pile of clean clothes: a folded scarf, a blue shirt with badges and epaulettes, a pair of wool socks with a red stripe, some yellowing cotton briefs that I wish I hadn't seen. "I'll have another load ready this afternoon," Pop reports. I can't help thinking about Greenie, who is the only other person I know who manages the laundry with this sort of devotional fervor. I don't know how it started, but by the time I was old enough to notice, my dad did a load a day, folding it in front of whatever Eagles, Flyers, or 76ers game was on TV. Sometimes, when the hamper was light, my mother would lean in my bedroom door and ask, with a genuine plea in her voice, "Do you have any clothes for your father? A towel? He's dying to do a load." She always said that a man needs a way to feel important around the house. I guess everyone already knows that mothers are irreplaceable.

"Thanks, Pop. Just in time," Evan says.

Pop smiles, gratified. "Well, you have your jamboree this weekend, right?"

"*Quest*. Right. Thanks."

While Evan takes his clothes out to his room, I flip through a booklet he left by the TV and realize that Evan is a Boy Scout. In Australia, it's called Rovers, but I can tell by the photos in this booklet that it's Scouting. Based on the chart, it looks like Evan is some kind of super Rover, like an Eagle Scout, which contradicts the image I've developed of him as lost and underemployed but clever enough to tackle a transmission. EACH INDIVIDUAL IS THE PRINCIPAL AGENT IN HIS OWN DEVELOPMENT, it says in bold letters across the bottom of every page. In the winter, there's something called Snow Moot. In the spring, Mudbash. What if he wants to show me his photos from Snow Moot '91? What if he asks me to be his date for Mudbash '92?

Back in my room, where it's dark enough to pass for midnight, I use a wood pole to push up the plywood that covers the skylight, wincing as I wiggle the board loose. Eventually, it sticks in place, letting the light fill the room. I stand back, thinking there must be a better way, something safer and more permanent . . . magnets, hinges, a hook. I add this to a list of Improvements to the Tanners that I've started in my journal.

> Hem Milly's nightgown
> Clean living room walls

Spot-clean velvet armchairs
Secure skylight cover
Forget Evan

By which I mean *Don't get sucked in. Fix what you can and get back out there to the distant shores.*

The weekend is here, and thank God for that. I've been going crazy, padding around in the blue hush of the Tanners. It's like living in a school library, the way we all tiptoe around, keeping conversation to a minimum. All week, I kept thinking of my brothers barreling through the back door, finding my mom and me in silence at the kitchen table, and saying, "Whoa, who died?"

At the pub, everyone's talking about Euro Disney, which opened this week.

"I reckon that's America's biggest export—the big mouse," our bartender says, tilting a pint glass under the tap. A guy with a shabby goatee drops the line that everyone's quoting, that Euro Disney is "a cultural Chernobyl," and I can tell by his tone that he thinks Americans are common philistines. "It's basically intellectual pollution," Goatee Boy says, looking at Tracy and me, waiting for a response.

A jolt of patriotism kicks in, and I can't *let it lie,* as my mother would advise. "I read in the paper that they hired like twelve thousand people," I say. "And, seriously, how evil can it be? It's roller coasters and cotton candy."

"Like Australia's Wonderland!" the bartender jumps in, guiding us back to conviviality. Tracy orders two more beers—Budweisers this time—and we move to a communal table where we can roll our eyes and meet better people.

"To Donald Duck," I say, raising my glass to hers.

"Cheers!"

In no time, we meet some boys, better boys, boys who agree that America and Australia are basically in-laws now that Tom Cruise married Nicole Kidman. We teach them to play Thumper, our favorite drinking game from college. People love making up signs and doing the motions and having to drain their beer every time they screw up. There's a lot of flirting, all harmless. Around one A.M., Tracy and I peel off and head back to the Tanners'.

Inching our way up the hill, we share the last cigarette, declaring it a Mega Night. In the unlit driveway, we walk quietly past Pop's window and into a mesh of fresh spiderwebs. We're covered in threads. We reach around for branches to break up the elaborate, invisible screen that secures the Tanner driveway at night. It's been years since I went to a Haunted House but the correlation is immediate.

While we brush our teeth, Tracy says, "Don't you hate it when people take digs at America?"

"Bugs the crap out of me," I say through a mouthful of toothpaste. "I don't even care if some of it's true." I spit toothpaste foam into the running water.

Before this year, I'd barely considered what it meant to be an American, other than my mother's dictate that good Americans buy U.S. products made on U.S. soil by U.S. workers. (For the bulk of my childhood, she piloted a wood-paneled Chevy wagon, flinging dirty looks at anyone behind the wheel of a Toyota or a Honda. *Honestly, who do they think gets their money and what do they think they're doing with it?*)

Around Main Line Philadelphia, my association with my mother felt unfavorable, unbearable, and, considering she was as beyond my control as American foreign policy, unfair. But when I was in middle school, the very zenith of self-consciousness, a nervy boy named Harry Morrison who liked to hang around my brothers but didn't like my mother's house rules (and wasn't afraid to give her the finger behind her back) took a potshot at her, and a dormant allegiance rose in me.

One night when no one was around, Harry Morrison took a can of black spray paint to the concrete underpass leading to our street and wrote in giant letters:

THE WITCH IS HAVING A SALE! BROOMS $1!

SUPPLIES LIMITED—ACT NOW

168 WOODED LANE

I read the announcement twice before I understood what it meant. "Oh my God, Mom."

"That's nice," she said coolly as we drove past it.

"That's YOU."

"Sticks and stones, Kelly. We don't worry about that sort of thing."

I worried about that sort of thing. I was thirteen; that was pretty much all I worried about. What did people think about me? What did they think of my mother—her nylon sweatsuit, her frosted hair, the way she cracked her gum? Last and most important, did what they thought of my mother make them think less or more of me?

"What are you going to do about it?" I asked, my voice shrill with panic.

"Absolutely nothing."

Some *foul-mouthed* kid who didn't like to be told to clean up his language or go home? Who wasn't invited to stay for dinner after rolling his eyes at her? That kid and his graffiti tantrum didn't bother my mother *one iota*.

In a matter of days, the message was covered by a sloppy black rectangle, but when the sun angled in, you could still see our address. On bad days, when I'd had a blowup with my mother over cutting my hair in her bathroom and clogging her sink, or using a certain dismissive tone with her that she *wouldn't use to talk to a criminal,* I'd think maybe Harry Morrison had it right. More often, I felt a strange, powerful mix of pity and chemical anger. It was my first taste of protective wrath, the kind that only mothers are said to possess.

It's still dark when Milly wakes up. I can hear her out there opening cabinets, so I roll out of bed and head to the kitchen.

"Hi," I say, turning on the overhead light.

"Hi."

"Want some toast?"

"No."

"Oatmeal?"

"No."

"Cereal?"

She sits down and looks at her reflection in the kitchen window. "My hair isn't long enough."

"What? I love your hair."

"It's ugly, and it won't stay up."

"I can braid it. I can French-braid it. Have you ever tried that?" She shakes her head. "Well, if you want, get a hairbrush and a ponytail holder, and I'll see what I can do."

My mom and I did not do this sort of thing. She had neither the inclination nor, as far as I know, the skill for hair design, and she was on high alert for vanity's handmaidens: blow dryers, hot curlers, special bands and accessories. The only exception I can recall was the night before my First Communion, when she told me to take a shower and meet her in her bathroom. She had a vision. I did as I was told and reported to her door. She led me in, sat me on the counter, and for the next fifteen minutes labored over me, slowly dividing my wet hair into sections, twirling the sections into tiny buns, clipping the buns to my head with two silver hairpins crisscrossed. We did not talk, but I knew she was happy because she made the same satisfied working noises she made when she polished silver or pulled flagging leaves off her potted plants, and because I saw her face in the mirror as she wrapped my head under one of her many navy blue/kelly green scarves and she was grinning. In the morning, she slipped out the pins two by two, and then it was time to shake out the curls. *Voilà!* she said. I put on my flouncy dress and buckled my hard, shiny shoes and stood in front of my mom, who looked at me and nodded. I could have tap-danced all the way to St. Thomas of Villanova, her attention made me so giddy. On the ride to church, I stared at myself in the side-view mirror, going on about my perfect hairdo as I ran my finger in and around the curl closest to my ear, until my mother turned around, her expression firm. *Remember, Kelly, today is about the good Lord, so let's focus our thoughts on Jesus and Mary.* She had gotten carried away and she regretted it.

When Milly comes back, I take her to my room, sit her on the floor between my knees, and brush through her shampoo-commercial hair, careful not to pull or rip a single strand, nothing that might make her repeal the privilege. She's given me a chance to solve a problem, and if I can do it—if I can make her like herself again—we will be closer.

I begin her braid and it builds into the perfect repeating weave of a Goodyear tire. There are no bumps, no sticky-outies. She wants to see. I open my closet door and turn her shoulders so she can admire her reflection in the mirror.

"I like it."

"I'm glad," I say, enjoying a rush of whatever hormones make you feel good as I tie it off with a pink rubber band.

"Yeah, I like it," she says again.

"Good."

"Can you do it again tomorrow?"

Tomorrow and every day after. "Sure."

"Okay, good." And she runs out of my room, touching the braid, looking for someone to show.

I turn around, flush with satisfaction and optimism. I can do this. I can help this girl. I can uncover every way there is to make her happy, to make her say *mmm*. Buy her pretty barrettes, keep her up late watching movies, have the Emmas over for a three-day party.

But then, on my dresser, I see a box of tampons, and I'm stopped short. Who will tell Milly about periods? That's no kind of work for a father. But who else will be here all those years from now to steer her through the fun house of puberty? Who will sit Milly down, as my mother did with me, and say, "I want you to know . . . well, I want to ask you . . . do you have any questions . . . about *anything*?"

"Like what?" I asked.

"Like," she said, straightening pens and pencils on her desk, "like . . . where babies come from."

"Mom, I'm sixteen!"

"I'm just asking—" She polished a letter opener on her sweater. "So . . . nothing at all?"

I *had* noticed something in the Reilly master bathroom the last time I babysat. "Okay . . ." I hesitated. "Well, yeah, there is one thing."

"Oh?" She looked uneasy.

"Yeah. What's a douche?"

"Oh, Kelly!" She shrieked like I'd put a centipede on her leg. "That is dis-GUS-ting!"

"It is? Even Summer's Eve?" I pictured the pretty lady on the box walking through a bright forest in a very clean sundress.

"Blech." She lowered her voice. "If you must know, a douche is something you squirt in your privates if they get dirty, which yours won't, so let's not get too involved in a discussion about douches. God almighty!" She turned her back to me. "And to think Susan Reilly is Catholic!"

Recalling this tête-à-tête with my mother, I'm inspired to write up a point-blank puberty cheat sheet for Milly. Bras, deodorant, zit management; pads, tampons, rubbers, and—though I was haunted by the image of a product that power-cleaned dirty vaginas—douches. But it's not my place. I'm a temp. Anyway, you probably can't get a kid from girlhood to womanhood with a one-page summary. It probably takes years.

Milly has dance class after school; I'm taking her while John blasts the soundtrack of *Fiddler on the Roof* and finishes painting the trim along the back of the house.

"Milly!" I call across the school playground, holding a bag with all her dance stuff. "You ready?" When she reaches me, her cheeks are flushed from running and the hair she thinks is so inadequate has fallen from either side of this morning's French braid, my big fix undone already.

"I need a hair band," she says in her queen-mum accent, which sometimes makes me feel crass and poorly educated.

"Do you want me to do another braid?" I take out the hairbrush I brought, and she takes it.

"No." My access to her has been revoked. This morning was

a fluke. "I'm fine." Milly yanks the brush through her hair while I stand there, resisting the considerable urge to step behind her and untangle her hair, working from the ends up to the roots like my mother made me.

In the lobby of the dance studio, Martin is quiet, lost in a confrontation between a handful of plastic horsemen and foot soldiers—*Torture! Kill! Die!*—his tone inappropriately cheerful, as usual. A few mothers page through magazines; one does her bills, ripping checks off the pad with terrific purpose.

Through a glass window, I watch Milly turn her feet out in arabesque. She's short on balance, but she grins as she holds her pose, glancing at friends around the room. Seeing her at ease fills my chest, like I've inhaled a hit of her mood. I've felt sorry for people before—I spent four years in college dorm rooms, trading sob stories over Domino's and Diet Coke—but feeling another person's joy like this is a new kind of empathy.

On the way out of class, I hand Milly her bag, along with her copy of *The Seven Wonders of the World,* a recent go-to.

"Thank you, Keely," she says casually, like she doesn't hate me at all.

"My brother has that book," says some girl in a tracksuit. "That's a boy book."

"What?" Milly asks, looking stung.

"That book—it's for boys," the girl says as she heads to the swinging door. "Boy boy boy."

"She's crazy," I say to Milly. "The Seven Wonders? Everyone loves the Seven Wonders."

Milly doesn't look at me. "Here, you take it," she says, shoving the book at Martin and pushing through the other girls to get to the front door.

I grind my teeth as Tracksuit Girl skips (skips!) down the

sidewalk in front of us, swinging off her mother's arm. I want to barrel after them and grab the girl's shoulders and scream into her snotty face, *You know what's boy boy boy? Tracksuits!*

For better or worse, I've latched on to Milly's ecosystem. What happens to her happens—in some weird refracted way that seems slightly dangerous—to me, too. And it occurs to me that maybe the reason my mother was so exhausted all the time wasn't because she was doing so much but because she was feeling so much.

By the time Evan comes in with the morning paper and a pencil, I've knocked out six letters. I fold my last blue aerogram and run the glossy edge across my tongue.

"Hey," he says, dropping down next to me.

"Hey." I tuck the envelope addressed to Mom Corrigan into the center of the pile. "How was Rovers?"

"Good, yeah. So, you ever play chess?"

"No. Backgammon . . . Rummy 500 . . . Spit." Spit makes him flip on a high-beam smile that's so much flashier than the rest of him. "You don't know Spit? It's a good game!"

"Yeah. So is chess. Want to learn?"

"Sure."

He puts an ottoman between us and sets up a board. He explains that there are sixty-four squares, eight by eight. He shows me the bishops and rooks, and tells me which pieces move diagonally, which by alley. He uses the words *blockade, obstruct, isolate.* I like them all, the way they sound, their metaphoric quality.

"This is your queen, your most essential piece. Only the queen has full range, meaning she can move in multiple directions. So always be aware of her and protect her. Once she's gone, it's a whole different game," he explains, like someone who remembers well the pain of losing his queen.

"You write a lot of letters," he says as he slides a pawn forward.

I pick the same pawn on my side and mirror his move.

"I'm a junkie for mail," I say.

"You get a lot of letters back?"

I shrug. "Not really." In the beginning, I heard from lots of friends, but eventually they went back to their lives, and now the only people who write regularly are my parents. My mom pens three or four letters for every one my dad scratches out. "So I'm pretty much just moving pawns. Should I be doing more?" I ask, switching topics.

"It's slow in the beginning. Your mum must write," he switches back, calling her out in a way that startles me.

"Oh, yeah."

"What's she like?"

"My mom? She doesn't play chess, I can tell you that. She likes other games—backgammon, bridge. Actually, I always think of her when you bring in the newspaper. She's big on the crossword, too. She does it while she has her Sanka."

"Is that medication?" he says, moving another pawn.

"Sanka? No, it's like coffee . . . fake coffee . . . coffee crystals."

He wants to know more about my mother, so I go on, even though the ground around this subject feels slippery.

"She spends a long time with the morning paper in general. She looks at the bridge hand, she checks her stocks, she does the Jumble—your paper doesn't have that—and then she goes to church and, after that, to work." I look at the board, wanting to do something bold and maybe regrettable—move the rook, slide the bishop out—something to match this conversation.

"What's her job?"

"She sells houses." I chicken out and move another pawn.

"What else?" He's hungry for details.

"Oh, I don't know. She's smart, or so my dad says. Big reader.

She's the one who told me to read the book I'm reading now, *My Ántonia*." He moves a rook. I decide to go big. "Was your mom into books?" I ask, looking up at him.

I don't look away, even though I feel shivery and unsure. A piece of his hair falls by his cheek and I have the urge to tuck it behind his ear. Nothing at all happens for a second, and then he meets my eyes. "Yeah." This is the first time we've held each other's gaze, and I am charged with affection for him. After a beat, he picks up his knight. "See, up two and over one. Or I could have gone over one and up two." Chess is not going to be my game. Too many choices, too many subtleties.

"Okay, then, so, I'm going to try this," I say, sliding my rook, impatient for action. We play for a while in silence. He doesn't remind me to keep an eye on my queen or ask me any more questions about my mom, and I don't ask him any more about his, and after about ten minutes he looks at the clock.

"Hey, I probably ought to get a shower before work. Do you mind if we leave things here and come back later?" He stands.

"Of course. That's a lot of ground to cover for one day."

He moves the board to a safe place.

"It gets easier to understand. You'll figure it out," he says, even though I think we both know I won't.

"Hi, I'm picking up mail," I say, setting my open passport on the American Express counter.

The clerk disappears. I smile at her colleague, who took care of me last week. I may be a bold girl, jumping continents, Paul Revering that *Things happen when you leave the house,* but I can't wait for news from home, even the most ordinary stuff. Is Booker's lacrosse team gelling? Did GT take that headhunting job? If so, what is headhunting?

The clerk finally returns with two letters: one from my grandmother, one from my mom.

"Nothing else?"

"Not today, Ms. Corrigan."

My grandmother tells me that Slugger is still dating May, which hardly seems worth mentioning after almost three decades. The Orioles started playing in their new stadium. My parents came down for a lovely visit. Jesus loves me.

My mom, sounding like a proctor from a Dickens novel, asks how *the children* are. She doesn't approve of "kids." *Kids are goats, Kelly. Are they goats?* She gives me lots of updates, as requested. GT started a rock-and-roll band. Booker's team is undefeated. She saw Amy at the Acme; she's getting serious with a Penn grad named John. Charlie is still in Russia, doing some kind of banking thing. My mom loves Charlie because one time she watched while he wagged his finger at me and said, "Your mom . . . your mom is the rudder."

I sit outside the American Express office with my letters on my lap. The lineage between my mother's handwriting and her mother's is clear, same *Y* and *G* and *Q*, just the way the nuns taught them. They vote for the same people, shop in the same department stores, serve the same hors d'oeuvres, and whisper the same prayers to the same God at night. They buy the same cigarettes, and when they light up they have the same detached expression, as if they could give up smoking at the snap of a finger. And they like a clean, well-behaved child who doesn't touch the furniture after it's been polished.

There are a few critical differences, my mom would rush to point out. Libby never drove a car. Not once. And unlike my mother, Libby had Josephine to clean and cook and do the laundry. Still, in matters that define, it's a straight line from my grandmother to my mother.

The connections between my mom and me are more like the webs crisscrossing the Tanners' driveway—flimsy and nearly invisible. In twenty-four years, there's been one and only one person who thought our affinity was obvious: Sharon, the receptionist at my mother's real estate office. Over my first Christmas break from college, my mom got me a job there answering phones. Six dollars an hour, five hours a day for two weeks—total gold mine.

"You must be Mary's daughter," said Sharon as I approached the front desk. "You look just like her!"

I don't look anything like my mother. We have literally nothing in common.

When a man walked in, Sharon called out, "Jim! This is Mary's daughter. Doesn't she look just like her? Jim, look at her.

Doesn't she look just like Mary?" Jim was head down in a contract of some sort. "Your mother is the life of the office," Sharon said to me, ignoring Jim ignoring her. "She's hysterical."

Hysterical? I'd started college four months ago. Could my mother have become hysterical in four months? Perhaps Sharon meant literally hysterical, as in unhinged. My dad had recently lost his job, and my mom was working again for the first time since her twenties. Maybe three college tuitions were making her hysterical. Or it might have been her empty nest. Maybe she was cracking under the invisible weight of new silence and empty space.

Eventually, Sharon gave me my instructions, and I settled in. But all day, all week, people kept stopping by my desk, interrupting my scrapbook project, to tell me about my mother.

"Oh, Mary, what a crack-up."

"That Mary C., she makes sure we don't take ourselves too seriously around here."

"She's a trip!"

Toward the end of the week, I was back in the break room buying a Diet Dr Pepper when I heard my mom say, "Yesterday at the brokers' open, I heard a great joke." I froze, like you would if you heard your mother flatulate or let out a peel of ecstasy behind a closed door. My mom didn't do those things, nor did she tell jokes. As far as I knew, she didn't know how.

"Well, one Christmas," she started, pulling her audience in, "sweet Janie Smith was worrying about what to give the mailman for a gift . . . a plant? a batch of cookies? She checked with her husband, who said, 'Screw him, give him a dollar.' So, the next morning, when the mailman arrived, Janie answered the door in her raciest lady-wear"—Sharon clucked, *Oh la la!*— "and invited the mailman in. She took him by the hand and led him upstairs to the master bedroom, where she treated him to a first-class lay, after which, Janie cooked the mailman a mouth-watering platter of eggs Benedict. Before he left, she handed him a single dollar bill. The mailman, confused but polite, thanked her. As he walked to the door, he turned back and said, 'Mrs. Smith, this has been a perfectly perfect morning—the lovemaking, the gourmet breakfast—but I gotta ask, what's going on here?' " My mother delivered the punch line in the dippy voice of Janie Smith. "Well, when I asked my husband what to give you for Christmas, he said, 'Screw him, give him a dollar!' The eggs Benedict was my idea."

The Realtors erupted. The joke landed. My mom held a crowd with a bit about screwing out of wedlock. I couldn't have been more disoriented. All my life my mother was my mother, nothing more. Not Greenie's saving grace, not the funny woman in the office.

But now I see there's no such thing as *a* woman, *one* woman. There are dozens inside every one of them. I probably should've figured this out sooner, but what child can see the women inside her mom, what with all that Motherness blocking out everything else?

John came home yesterday with four tickets to Australia's Wonderland. The kids wanted Evan to go, but that was never going to happen. Then they asked if Pop could come, and John laughed and explained that the fourth ticket was for me, which made Martin bounce on his tiptoes and Milly sulk off to her room. After a tease of a breakthrough, her opposition is back in force.

We start the day on the Scooby-Doo merry-go-round, which Milly is so beyond that just waiting for her brother to take his turn offends her. We parade from there down a long path under a striped canopy past the Bam Bam Ball Pit, which, Milly notes, is "for babies," to bumper cars, which are, thankfully, "Brilliant!" On Milly's command, she and Martin ambush me. For all the times she's wanted to carve me up with every heinous word she knows, me and the entire adult world that has replaced her top-quality mother with a ninny of a nanny, I say, *Bring it on*. She's too young to box or split wood. I hope it helps. But after a few minutes of them ramming me from both sides, John reins her in.

By lunch, moods are dipping. It's broiling. Martin's hairline is wet. Milly stares at the goo on the tip of the ketchup bottle, making me wonder how long it's been sitting here and how many grubby hands have touched it. Here comes John with a tray of fried food, his forehead dripping. In the photographs on the brochure, no one is sweating, and all the tables are clean. Families of four eat fresh fruit and drink milk while mums and dads share satisfied looks over their children's heads.

On the way to the gondola after lunch, we pass a doddering Captain Caveman. Milly waves, and Martin leans in for a hug.

"If you give me your camera," I say to John.

"Right."

I take their photo. In this light, the shutter opens and closes in a thousandth of a second. And for that thousandth of a second, the Tanners look full of life. That's how this outing will be recorded. *Look at this one!* they'll say decades from now. *Oh, that was a great day.* But I can't tell if John is really here or not. He smiles on command, ginning up cheeriness as best he can, buying lollies and chocolates for everyone, but when I lower the camera, his cheeks drop.

On the monorail ride to Hanna-Barbera Land, I raise the topic of Evan with John, looking for some insight into their discord.

"So how long has Evan been living in the garage?"

"Long time," John says, surveying the park below.

"Always," Martin says.

"He pays rent," John wants me to know.

"He's really been helpful," I want him to know.

John considers his response, weighing out how blunt he can be. I raise my eyebrows just enough to say, *Go ahead, tell me,* but he abstains.

"Good," he says with firm punctuation, reminding me of my mother saying, *If you can't say something nice, keep your fat mouth shut.*

Inside the park's theater, we buy tickets for a stage performance that brings together Yogi Bear, the Tasmanian Devil, and Australia's favorite bad boy, Ned Kelly. John's energy picks up, probably because of the air-conditioning, though I've noticed he loves a musical.

After the show, we make our way to the flume ride, where the line folds back on itself many times. People lean heavily on the handrails and linger under the eucalyptus trees for shade. Many men have their shirts off, several of whom should not. Parents around us refocus their kids' attention from the long wait to the big payoff to come—*Just a few more minutes! Look at that drop!* Being a kid is all about learning to bide time, proving just how unnatural it is to delay gratification.

"This was my favorite when I was little," I say.

"You came here?" Martin asks, making the mother in front of us in line smile.

"No, we have these in America, too. Every spring vacation, my parents took us to this place called Busch Gardens."

"Every vacation!" Martin repeats breathlessly, like I've said we lived in a tree with elves and pet squirrels.

"My dad sold ad space in a women's magazine, so we got free family passes," I explain to John.

"Free!" Martin says, looking at his dad for some sort of visual confirmation that he, too, is hearing this astonishing news, but John has dropped out of the conversation, so I just keep talking to Martin, the only one who's trying hard enough to have a good time.

Finally, it's our turn. Milly pulls her dad beside her, so Martin comes to me. We sink into our seats and the safety bars drop. A teenager in an Australian Wonderland polo shirt walks backward, giving each bar a quick jiggle. An announcement runs through the loudspeakers, and then the operator leans forward on a lever, and we're jerked out of the shed and into the day-light.

All the tension of the ride is tied to that first crawl up the ramp, metal on metal, gears grinding. The bold and the brave shout, "Here we go!" waving their hands over their heads. The others, pale and tight-lipped, grip the handles and lean into their parents, burying their faces.

We reach the top. Martin takes my hand. We look at each other as we tilt over the pinnacle and scream as we plummet down the chute. We're yanked around the track, closer and closer to the final drop, where we will be soaked through and look like all the waterlogged families we saw cackling and pull-ing their wet shorts off their thighs as they filed out. As we free-fall, a wall of water comes over the bar and into our laps and Martin screams out, *Mummy!* An instant later, the boat is righted and he is snapped back into today, and although I know Milly heard his glaring, forgivable, heartbreaking *Mummy!*—and al-though this is just the kind of reckless transference she has worked so hard to prevent—not a word is said about it. In fact, as we exit the ride, she sidles up beside him and takes his hand, making something clear for the first time: She will look after Martin, better than anyone.

Before John leaves for New Zealand, he gives me grocery money and an apology for not stocking the kitchen himself. I try to tell him not to worry, I can go to the store, but he doesn't know—or can't remember—how to hand things over.

At the market in St. Leonards, the cereal selection is the same as back home, though they've put koalas and kangaroos on all the boxes. I pass on the chocolate cartoon garbage and reach for Shredded Wheat, my mom's go-to. In the raw food section, I load up on berries and dried fruits and three kinds of nuts. If the kids won't eat it, the Rover will. I toss a box of graham crackers in the cart for Martin, whose puppy affection makes me feel magnanimous. In the refrigerated section, ground chuck is on special. I decide, after standing there with the door open too long, *like I think electricity grows on trees,* to buy five pounds. I can divide it up into burgers and freeze them, like my mom used to. (Once or twice a month after a sale, she'd pull a block of anemic brown turds from the freezer, slap it against the Formica to break the patties apart, and *voilà!*—dinner for five.)

In the shampoo aisle, I slow down to find a mousse Tracy told me about, but I'm distracted by the rows of hair dye, something I've never tried. Each shade is displayed on a twist of shiny plastic hair that sticks off the shelf like a tongue. Deepest Mahogany, Sassy Amber. My mom, usually a blonde, went red once. I remember seeing a photo of her posing with her monogrammed tote bag in London. She was young—my age, actually—and pregnant with GT. She wore crisp cotton pedal pushers over her belly, and had trim ginger locks. I pick Scarlet Fire.

I turn down the baking aisle, and there, just ahead, is Eugenia Brown, the woman who sacked me.

I'm moving fast now. I can't wait to run into her.

"Eugenia? Is that you?" She looks up from the instant cake mix. "Kelly, it's Kelly," I say, prompting her, forcing her. "Remember? You hired me? Well, hired and fired." I don't know where this surge of cockiness is coming from, but I am hot to embarrass her. I glance around, hoping to draw in a witness to make it more awkward.

She smiles tentatively. "Oh, yes, hello."

"Hello to *you*! I'm just here shopping for my new family," I say, beaming. "Wonderful children. Great situation. Really love them." I'm on a roll.

"Oh, that's good," she says.

"It's better than good. It's fantastic! We make such a good team. They are just so"—I pause, flipping through attributes, looking for something with just the right bite—"grateful!"

"All right, well, I better keep moving."

I stand square to her, pulsing with out-of-control bravado. "I hope you were able to find a suitable replacement. A young Asian, isn't that who you said worked out best for you?"

"We're fine," Eugie Brown says, looking angry now. "Good day."

I may have gone just a touch too far. "Okay, well, tell the kids I said hello! Richard, too."

In the checkout line, I salute myself. I am a competent individual, a freethinker, a force. No one works me over!

But while I load the grocery bags into the back of the van, I catch sight of myself in the side mirror and realize that I don't look so much like an independent woman as I do a barely distinguishable version of my mother on any given day of the seventies or eighties—snubbing sugar cereal, stockpiling hamburger meat, sorting through hair dyes, demanding eye contact, standing down the occasional adversary. Even more surprising is that the recognition of her in me does not give me pause. Here, in this moment, I find the likeness kind of exhilarating.

I'm up early, making lunches, when Milly finds me in the kitchen working on her sandwich.

"That's too much," she says, looking at the Vegemite. "You always put too much." If you ask me, any Vegemite is too much Vegemite.

"Why didn't you tell me?"

"Because I'm not allowed to complain."

Oh, this girl and the list of things she can't do or say. *I hate my nanny. I cry at night. I'm not okay.* How much make-believe can a seven-year-old take?

I spread as thin a layer of Vegemite as has ever been applied to a piece of bread, barely a stain, and hold up my work for inspection.

"Not enough. I can do it myself. I'm almost eight."

I hand over the butter knife and reposition the cutting board in front of her. She drags the knife forcefully across the dry bread, which rolls up and breaks, as I knew it would. In the most pitiful way, her failure pleases me.

"This knife is bad," she says.

"Tell me about it."

"Tell you what?"

"Nothing. It's an expression."

"A what?"

"An expre— Nothing."

While she works on her second piece, I check my desire to meddle, to fix, and maybe, glory of all glories, to save. Intervention will backfire. Milly is a sovereign state.

"So, what do you want for dinner?" I ask.

"Um, soup," she says.

"Soup?" I didn't eat soup until I was in college.

"Soup."

"What kind?"

"The kind you make in a pot. From in a cookbook." She points to the shelves behind me.

I've never made soup or been in a kitchen where soup was being made. Restaurants make soup. People open cans, or they go to restaurants where soup is made.

I pull out the most likely resource, a thick book covered in faded blue linen called *New South Wales Favourites,* and flip around in the "Soups & Sauces" section. Crumbs fall from the pages. Then, in the margin of page 26, next to the ingredients for "Fall's Best Minestrone," I see handwriting—delicate, easy, feminine—perfectly matching the composite I've created of Ellen Tanner in my imagination. This is as real as she has felt to me, as if she stood in this exact spot only a moment ago, so present that if I knew how to parse the smells of this house, I'm sure I could pick up her scent.

Her note—to whom, I wonder—next to *pasta shells* says, *Use barley here.*

"So, okay, here's one," I say with hesitation. "Minestrone. Do you like minestrone?"

"Yes, with barley."

"Ah."

To me. The note was to me, I guess.

"When is Daddy coming home?" Milly asks when I pick her up from school, sounding like me for the first ten, or twenty, years of my life.

"Around dinnertime." I reach over to put on her seat belt but she shakes me off. She's got it.

"That's so long from now," she whines.

I've done a fine job these last two days, but the kids miss John all the same. Even if he sometimes seems lost or out of place, more like a stepfather than a father, the kids want him more than anyone. I guess that's the thing about parents.

"How do you like my new hair? I dyed it."

"Your hair died?" Martin asks.

"No, I colored it. I made it red with a dye, like tie-dyed shirts."

"It doesn't look red," Milly says, meeting my eyes in the rearview mirror. She's right. It doesn't look anything like the plastic hair in the supermarket. Some things you can't change.

As we pull out, I turn on the radio. "Okay, guys. This is Tom Petty." I jack up the volume. "Listen. Hear that organ?" I raise my finger and tap it in the air. "'. . . *Said a woman had hurt his pride . . .*'" I turn it up louder, maybe louder than this radio has ever been played. "'*Don't do me like that . . .*'"

"Do me like what?" Milly asks.

"And what means *pride*? How does it hurt?" Martin wants to know, challenging me to rephrase the line using only the words a child will understand.

"It just means you feel dumb, someone made you feel stupid."

"By hurting you?"

"Sorta. Just listen to the song." I sing a little louder.

There's so much to define and differentiate. As I stutter through a definition of terms, I wonder if John and Ellen used all the big hard words, like *tumor, neurosurgery, chemotherapy,* or just kept it simple. *Boo-boo. Owwie. Yucky medicine.*

"Stop!" Milly shouts from the back.

"Stop!" Martin calls. "Keely!"

"Aw, come on, this is a great song!" I call back over my shoulder, belting out the refrain.

"No!" Milly barks.

"Dammit! I just went the wrong way!" I am now on the Pacific Highway, which is dramatic and curvy, like the roads in BMW commercials.

"Move over!" Martin shouts as I accelerate into the turn, leaning forward, hoping for an exit sign.

"No!" Milly screams. "Stop!"

"Hey! Not another word," I say, verbatim Mary Corrigan. "Not another word!"

"Keely! Keely!" A car beeps.

"Shhh!" Another car beeps.

Two cars are driving straight toward us.

"We're on the wrong side!"

"Oh God!" I swerve, prickling with adrenaline. "Oh God." I flip off the radio, turn on my hazards, and pull over to the shoulder, my breath caught in my throat.

"I'm so sorry. Thank you. I thought . . . Thank you. I'm so sorry." I put on the emergency brake and wait for the rush to pass, to feel safe and competent and level again. I slipped into autopilot. I forgot I was in a new place, with different rules and people who don't belong to me.

Eventually, I start a five-point turn, inching myself around, letting many cars pass, waiting for an opening in the traffic that poses no risk whatsoever. We drive home slowly, quietly, like we're crossing a gorge on a wire.

John is smart not to rely on me. This isn't some lark. I'm driving around, playing the music too loud, ignoring the signs and shushing the warnings, with a man's last and best treasure in the backseat. The teetering height of this truth, its shadow with no end, gives me vertigo.

That evening, John returns from his travels. The kids give him a hero's welcome, and for a moment anyway, the house feels lively. But once we sit down to dinner, the dialog track drops out and we eat to sounds, not words. Martin hums a made-up song as he chews, though not so loudly that we can't hear Milly's teeth breaking through her carrots. John cuts his meat all at once, like my mother told me never to do, his knife clicking and squeaking against the plate's surface. Pop works through his meal methodically, as if it's a lawn he's mowing, while Evan stands at the kitchen counter eating what he can in the minutes he has left before work. The five of them are not so much a family as its components, like Evan's Scirocco broken apart and spread out on the driveway. It's a complex machine requiring a level of coordination between connection points that not everyone is capable of. Maybe it will run again. Maybe it won't.

The lethargy around here is seeping into me. Since getting the kids off to school this morning, I've been drifting around, noting things that need attention without actually attending to them: crumbs on the counter from the morning's toast, chairs askew around the kitchen table that would make the whole house feel better if only they were tucked in, Martin's Ninja Turtles hat, the one he loved so intensely and then forgot existed, jammed in the cushions of the living room sofa. I should pull it out, reshape it, take it back to his room, hang it on a hook so it's waiting for him on the day he remembers his *favorite* hat. Instead, I just stare at it, too tired to move.

I drink tea, each cup a chance at a new beginning. *I'll have some chamomile, and then I'll sort out the kids' closet. After this cup, I'll do the beds. One more pot, and I'll take a shower.* Standing by the window, blowing, sipping, I stare out at the shady part of the lawn, still heavy with the night. It'll take hours for the sun to reach that patch, dry the beads of water clinging to each blade, and free the grass to spring back to its usual posture. There's no rushing some things.

By midday, I realize it's not the sleepy collective heart rate around here that's left me comatose. I'm sick.

My mom's a pro with aches and ailments. Unlike funks and malaise, physical problems draw her near. The lure of the fix. If she were here, she'd stick a thermometer under my tongue, check my swollen glands, jot down my temperature, give me two aspirin, and make me gargle warm salt water, all the while talking in the sugary lilt of a nursery school teacher. Before leaving me to rest, she'd spray Lysol around the room to kill every last germ, slather Vicks VapoRub under my chin, and wrap my neck in a piece of Egyptian cotton about the size of a tea towel that she keeps for just such occasions. I miss her, or I miss that part of her. I always do when I'm sick.

After I've spent a couple of hours wincing through every swallow, Evan sends me to an office in Beecroft, where Dr. Hannah takes a look at my throat and orders a culture. She says she's 99 percent sure it's strep and that I should call tomorrow to confirm.

The next morning, it's official. The nurse asks how many times I've been on antibiotics in the past couple years, and I'm not sure. "You don't know?" she asks, like, *How old are you? Twelve?* My mother would know. She's read all about antibiotic resistance. People are *too damn quick* to take drugs, and someday they're going to be *mighty sorry,* and that's not going to happen to her kids, not if she can help it. She writes all our prescriptions in a book that she keeps in her top desk drawer so she can put her finger on the information in two seconds. The nurse rephrases her question. "Do you recall taking any antibiotics in the past three years?" I say no.

After lugging myself home from the pharmacy, I come in the front door and Martin slides toward me on the floor like a seal at Sea World, his chest on a chair cushion. "Are you better?" he wants to know.

"No, but I will be," I say, shaking the prescription bag.

His eyes widen. "I know what that is! Mummy had those!"

"Oh, Martin." Tears come to my eyes.

Evan appears and sees me swallowing my emotion. "You okay?"

"Yeah, just strep, just a dumb cold," I say, looking at Martin.

"You sure?"

I nod.

"You should rest, read your book." Evan pats my arm, touching me for the first time since we shook hands two months ago.

"Yeah, tha— Wait, what's Martin doing home?"

"Mini-day today."

"Oh, God, right. Good thing you're here."

I slip into bed and fold my pillow in half behind me, just right for reading. Ántonia's father has died. The new world was too much for him. His family is moving on, finding shelter in a place with "very little broken ground." Work is their answer to the grief that keeps pounding to get in. No doubt that appealed to my mother, who considers action infinitely superior to analysis. Button up the kids, tidy the house, get dinner on and off the table by seven, that's the ticket. Examine? Share? Feel? *I'd rather do time at Montgomery County Correctional.*

I nod off after a few pages and dream that I'm trying to tell my mom about Evan and the kids—explaining who is step, who is half, how each is holding up—until she finally understands, and I am so happy that we make sense to each other for once that I shower her with gifts, first a turtle and then a teapot.

At the end of my dream, Evan taps on my door. He has warm salt water. Martin follows behind him with pink construction paper. "I made you a card!"

"Thanks. Hey, Martin, before I forget, I saw your Ninja hat. It's in the sofa, between the cushions."

"Yeah, Keely!" Maybe he's been missing it after all.

John comes home, and when Evan steps out into the hall to talk to him, I strain to hear the conversation. Their voices are low and soft. I've wanted to see them interact since the day I met Evan.

"I hear you're sick," John says, appearing in my doorway.

"Yeah, strep, but I started antibiotics, so I'll be fine."

"Let me get you some lozenges and ibuprofen," John volunteers. "Ev will get you some more warm salt water." *Ev,* he said. He called Evan *Ev,* like my dad calls me *Kel.*

"I still have some, thank you."

"Very good. We'll let you rest, then."

Some families are at their best camping, others making lasagna or playing charades. Ántonia's family blends together breaking land, driving cattle, harvesting crops. For my family, it was working the sidelines at lacrosse games and playing a card game called 99 that provided the ideal forum for trash talking. For the Tanners—and my mother—it's managing illness. Filling prescriptions, treating symptoms and side effects, keeping the house quiet, these are things they've done together, and it shows. They know how to care-take, and in taking care they are able to do things they otherwise can't: touch, collaborate, indulge. Even if, just like when I was young, all that gooey tenderness hardens as my temperature returns to normal, I saw it, I know it's there.

John mentions, as he's packing for another overnight, that he and the kids are planning a weekend away in a place called Avoca, which sounds like someone tossed the word *vacation* in the air and let it reinvent itself in a new but strangely familiar order.

"We have a place there." Nothing about John Tanner says *second home*. "We used to like to go quite a bit. We'd love for you to join us . . . if you like," he says without looking at me.

"Oh, wow, that's nice. Sounds great."

John turns and smiles, and for a moment I feel good, like I've given him something he needed. But the very next moment? Hesitation. And the moment after that? Regret. What are John Tanner and I going to talk about for two days? I can't even imagine the car ride.

"The kids will be happy you're coming."

"Even Milly?" I toss out, grinning, trying to convey an easy acceptance of my uneasy relations with his daughter.

"Has she— What do you mean?" He is genuinely puzzled.

"Oh, nothing, I'm just joking. I was just— She's so funny— I just need to . . . get her sandwich right."

What else hasn't he noticed?

After John leaves, Martin finds me and asks if I want to draw with him.

"Sure. What should we draw? Wait, I know, let's draw your house at the beach!"

"First do your house," he says.

Our house was and still is a two-story four-bedroom traditional, which is to say a box built around a central staircase. I draw a rectangle with shuttered windows, a chimney, and a front door right in the middle.

"Now draw your house that you're going to have when you get babies," he prompts.

"When I grow up?"

He thinks this is very funny. "Keely, you are grown up!"

"Sort of. Okay, so it'll probably be a lot like my parents' house." His smile sags. He was hoping for more. "But"—I add a large pond in the backyard—"with a place to swim in the summer and ice-skate in the winter." He likes that. Isn't that what we all want? A future that's familiar but a little better than what we knew as children?

"My house is not a box," Martin says, leaning over the paper, squeezing his pencil until his fingertips turn white. "It is like Legos."

"It probably was a box, then your sister and you came along, and they added your room; then Pop moved in, and they added his space." No one would design this layout from scratch. The awkward additions have made too many corners and dead ends, suited less for family time than for hide-and-seek.

"And Ev's room!"

"Oh, right, there's that, too."

After I finish, Martin holds our two drawings up toward the light and layers them. "Look, I can see yours through mine."

"That's cool," I say, looking at the outline of my childhood through the outline of his.

He wants to know where my room was and whether I shared with my brother like he shares his with Milly, and then he wants me to tell him a story. "About when you were five years old!"

"Oh, boy, let's see . . ." What story do I have for him? Something he'll relate to. "Hey, I have an idea! Let's make model houses. I saw some Popsicle sticks in a drawer this morning—" I divert him because honest to God, right at this moment, I can't think of one story that won't bring us straight to my mother, which is the real difference between the outline of his childhood and the outline of mine.

On the second morning of John's trip, Evan and I are deep into *Santa Barbara* when he says they should sell this season on video. "Just the best scenes, like the top ten."

"We could make serious money doing that," I say, accidentally putting a *we* out there. "How long have you been watching this, anyway?"

"Oh—well—" He freezes up like I've caught him in a trap. "A couple years."

Then it hits me. He watched this with his mother. I bet this was her show. I bet she used to sit in this chair. That's what people do when they're sick. They watch TV. I would. If I had a bad disease, I'd stay home in my softest pajamas, flip on some daytime drama, and crawl into another life until I fell asleep with someone else's problems filling up my head.

How much longer will Evan watch? A year? Forever?

After the show, Evan says he has stuff to do, but he'll be around at dinnertime if that's cool.

"Sure," I say, meaning *totally*. "I was going to make carbonara."

"The kids may not go for it, but it sounds great to me."

Before dinner, I tighten the straps on my bra to make my boobs look better, and rub lotion into my dusty arms. By the time

Evan comes in, I've already fed the kids—plain spaghetti, bacon on the side—and they're back in their room, working on a puzzle.

"I'm trying to get this sauce to thicken," I say.

"I'll do the table," he says, opening a side cabinet. He digs out two dinner plates, different from the ones we usually use. Pop passes by and runs his fingers across a plate without saying anything, and my guess is that I will never know any more about these obviously special plates than I do now, which is to say they carry some current that begs touching.

While the sauce thickens, I wander into the living room and pick through the rack of albums, which is dominated by musical soundtracks. I see an old Jackson Browne album that I memorized in high school. I tip the vinyl out of its sleeve, lay it on the record bed, and set the needle on the glossy edge. The first song is about lying in the tall grass with someone, filling otherwise empty hours, trading small comforts and, where necessary, mercy—like Ántonia and Jim and maybe like Evan and me. Next to the stereo, tucked to the side, is a photo of Ellen I missed when I first combed through the room. Her hair is short and soot-black, and she's surprisingly heavy, maybe two hundred pounds. All five of her children surround her.

"You want some wine?" Evan calls out from the kitchen. "There's a bottle open in the fridge."

"Sure." Now we're getting somewhere.

"I turned down the stove. I think it's good," Evan says as he comes into the living room, holding out a juice glass filled with Chardonnay.

"Classy."

He smiles, but when he sees what I'm looking at he shakes his head. "That wasn't her," he says defensively. "Her hair was growing back after surgery—she didn't like it dark like that. And she was never a big person. As part of her treatment, they put her on steroids, which made her swell up."

"She doesn't look bad." She looks awful. Who would take this photo? Who would keep this photo?

Evan digs in the drawer next to the sofa. He knows where to find the photo he likes. "Here," he says, holding out the picture of Ellen and Pop, the one I knew already. "This was her. I mean, her eyes are closed, but you can see she was pretty."

"Really pretty."

"Really pretty," he echoes, then sticks the unseemly image between two albums, not to be seen again until someone plays the soundtrack from *Oklahoma!* or *Mame.* "I don't know why John keeps that." I don't know, either, of course I don't, but maybe her mangy hair and bloated, distended body remind him of the awful side effects of her treatment, and that helps him think of his wife less as dead and more as free.

Over dinner, I babble about all the plans Tracy and I have for the rest of our travels. Evan says that by the time Tracy and I leave Australia for New Zealand, we will have seen more of his country than he has.

"I've been meaning to get out to the reef and up to Cape Trib," he says. "The timing just hasn't been right." He had lists, too. Exciting things he was going to do and see and learn. But then he got stuck here, doing and seeing and learning other things.

After dinner and dishes, before Evan's shift, we run aground on conversation, so we take the last of the wine over to the TV area and watch a sketch comedy show called *Fast Forward,* sort of like an Australian *Saturday Night Live*. A comedian named Chenille plays a tarty, self-assured entrepreneur selling a no-frills funeral service for the "budget-conscious bereaved." She explains that vertical stacking allows them to keep prices "low low low." I shrink back, so uncomfortable sitting next to Evan. When Chenille says they employ a "bevy of necro-cosmeticians" because "a lassie wants to look her best when she gets to the pearly gates," he laughs so hard that he practically chokes, loud enough to wake the neighbors. It's the most noise I've ever heard him make.

After my mother's brother, Uncle Tommy, died of cancer, I heard her laugh at the strangest things, like the apparently hilarious disgrace of puking into a bedpan. That made her laugh hard enough to cry. I wasn't even thirteen, I didn't know anything about anything, but I did understand that she was allowed to laugh because she had been there. She had seen it and this black humor was part of how she dealt with it.

I don't remember one day of Tommy being sick, and that's just fine with her. My mother has zero interest in exploring mortality—*that's what noon Mass and rosary beads are for*—and considers anything beyond the headline "My brother has a health issue" to be *hanging out private family business*.

The day of Uncle Tommy's funeral, I was a month away from starting high school. I remember coming down to the kitchen that morning.

"Where's Mom?" I asked GT.

"Packing for Baltimore," he answered flatly, holding everything in. He loved Tommy. We all did. Tommy was Princeton-smart and athletic. My brothers used to play pond hockey with him, and my dad always said Tommy moved on the ice like Fred Astaire in kneepads.

My mom's door was closed for most of the morning, so instead of being upbeat-cheerleader guy, my dad said all the stuff she usually said.

"Brush your teeth."

"No sneakers."

"Make sure you go to the bathroom before we get in the car."

When my mom came out of her room, the only thing on her that stood out was a gold pin. Everything else was black. She had on her usual makeup, except lipstick. I couldn't decide whether she was waiting to put it on until we got closer to Baltimore, or she forgot, or she got too tired to keep going. For all I knew, it was inappropriate to wear lipstick to your brother's funeral.

Before I could say anything, she looked down at me and said, "You used my hairbrush. I took out my hot rollers and picked up my brush and ran it through my hair, and it was all wet, and now my hair . . ." She petered out. The rest didn't matter. I looked at the carpet. She had told me three hundred times to stop touching her things, especially her hairbrush.

Downstairs, she took a new pack of cigarettes out of the carton in the kitchen drawer, even though once we got to my grandmother's there would be Benson & Hedges in silver boxes on every side table. My mom was going to smoke on the way down, and no one was going to complain.

I sat in the back of the station wagon with my mom's pillow, which I was not to touch. GT and Booker were in the middle. We went from one road to the next, our back-alley route to 95 South. At one point my dad said, "Not much traffic today," but no one responded. I didn't know where my brothers' electronic football games were, but they weren't making those *click-click-*

*click*s and we weren't checking sports scores on the radio. The only sound was the car lighter popping. My mom pinched her lips around a cigarette and pressed the red-hot coil into the tip and sucked while I watched from the backseat.

When she turned to look out the window, I could see her profile in a column of twisting smoke. She shivered, and a long tear slid down her cheek, which she caught as it drove toward the corner of her mouth. She slipped her finger under her large plastic sunglasses to stop the next one. For a minute, she made no noise at all, not even a breathing sound, and then her body took over and made her exhale. I had never seen her cry. I wanted to pat her back, but I couldn't reach.

After the service, on the church steps, I watched Tommy's widow and my cousins get into a black car. My mother stood nearby, letting people say things to her while she kept one eye on my dad, who was standing in a cluster of his brothers. One of them said something amusing, and they all chuckled. The moment my dad's laughter reached my mother, she was done.

"Wait here," she said to me, and headed for him with her open hand leading. "Gimme the keys. I have to get out of here. I can't stand this another minute."

My dad's brothers stepped back, and my dad looked down, same as I did that morning when I got in trouble for using her hairbrush.

The reception was at my aunt Regina's. I heard my father ask my mom if there was anything he could do, and she said, "All I care about is Mother. Make sure people don't wear her out. And when it's time to wind it down, let's wind it down. The last thing Mother needs is a houseful of people who won't leave." I told myself to remember that instead of watching TV upstairs with my cousins.

There was so much food at Tommy's house. More than I'd ever seen there. My mom didn't touch it. She stood near the foyer on a red Oriental carpet, greeting mourners. She kept her heels and earrings on the whole time and did the thing that is always the hardest for her: She made small talk.

Everyone asked about Regina and Libby, and my mom said, "They're tired. It's been a long, hard road."

"Cancer is so awful. I can't imagine my child . . ." they said.

"God help us," she replied, looking over at me.

We hung around all evening, until the last person left. After the table was cleared and wiped clean, we went to Libby's house. My mom trudged up the stairs, and I followed behind her. I tried to say something kind, but all I could think of was "Do you want a glass of water?"

She shook her head and sat down at the top of the stairs on a strange antique chair that looked like a royal commode. "Say a prayer for your cousins."

"I will."

The next morning, my brothers and I were up and out without any squabbling. We rode home to Philly without saying much, all in our own thoughts. Eventually, I fell asleep in the way-back, hugging my mother's pillow that smelled just like her, a heady mix of face powder, Final Net, and hand cream, understanding that my mom had lost someone she loved so much, someone important, and that made her different in an essential way from my father, who could still circle up outside a church, all his brothers in a line, and have a good long gab about nothing much.

I wake up the next morning feeling energetic, you might even say hale, so I decide to leave the car at home and pick up the kids on foot.

"We're *walking* home?" Martin asks in total disbelief, like the house was in Perth.

"Yes."

He stares at me. "Why didn't you come in the car?"

"I thought it would be fun to be outside on a nice day. I brought money to buy juices." I hold out a fiver.

"We're walking all the way to the market?" We're not even off school property yet.

"Come on, Martin, it's fun!" Milly says, aggravating him with her smarmy encouragement.

"No. It. Is. Not!" Martin says, stomping his feet in time to his protest.

"Don't be a baby!" she shoots back.

"I've got this, Milly," I say, eager to eliminate compounding elements. It's a minefield, this kid stuff.

"Why for, Keely?" Martin whines.

Thanks to my dumb idea about strolling home in the fresh air and sunshine, I am suddenly face-to-face with a deeply unsympathetic side of my only fan.

"Because it's good for you."

"Not for me it isn't good," he says to the sidewalk.

I could give him a piggyback, he's easy to carry—Milly's too big for anyone except John—but I should be firm, let him hate me for a few more minutes, show him who's steering this ship. That's what a real mother would do. That's what my mother would do.

"I like walking!" Milly says, practically skipping. She likes walking when her brother doesn't, *that's* what she likes. She likes being the Easy One for once. Even though her motive is obvious, I feel a surge of affection for her, along with an irrational hope that, from here on out, she will take my coaching, say thank you, allow me to console her. It's easy to love kids who make you feel competent. God help the ones who lock themselves in their rooms, who let go first, who make you pine for some sign of validation and then hate yourself for chasing the affections of a child.

Twenty-eight minutes into a walk that took me ten, we still have a hundred yards until we get to 3 Lewiston Street and I'm mad—mad that my good idea isn't working, mad that Martin has turned against me, madder still that I didn't understand this was inevitable. Of course he was going to turn on me, and over any little thing. I'm only as good as my last shark throw or grilled PB&J.

Finally, we reach the porch. Martin climbs the steps like a dying Bedouin. "Why did you do that?" he asks.

"All right already, God, Martin! We're home, okay?" I snap.

"Hey," Evan calls from the driveway. "Everybody okay?"

"Ev!" Martin runs to Evan. *Runs*.

"Yeah, it's just— It was a long walk home," I explain.

Evan loops an arm around Martin. "Come on, mate, help me clean out my tent."

"And do roly-poly bugs!" he squeals, invigorated. Martin is back.

"Yeah, we'll find a few in there."

"Roly-poly, roly-poly!" Martin chirps, instantly made whole by someone shiny and new. It's easy to make a kid love you if you give him whatever he wants. What was I supposed to do? Let Martin whine his way out of a short walk on a nice day? Hail a taxi?

Something about this strikes me as a key to the story of my mother and me. She often said that I was a different person for my father, that I'd do anything for him, without an ounce of backtalk, as upbeat as a Miss America contestant, and that by the time he got home at night all the fighting was over, so he never knew what it took to get me to turn off the TV or take out the trash.

She also said, *Lemme tell you something, Kelly, you changed me a lot more than I changed you.* I didn't know adults could be changed. I thought they were finished pieces, baked through and kiln-dried. I never understood that when we fought my mother was having actual emotional reactions. I assumed her behavior was a front—a calculated show—designed to yield the best and safest possible kid.

After a couple of months' suffering at Milly's mercy, still smarting from today's rejection by Martin, I see that, sturdy though my mother was, she must have been *gutted* by the sound and sight and sheer vibration of her rabid daughter roaring, *I HATE YOU! I HATE YOUR GUTS! I HATE YOU FOR-EVER!* I had thought a good mother would not elicit such comments, but now I see that a good mother is required to somehow absorb all this ugliness and find a way to fall back in love with her child the next day.

The Tanner beach house is north of Sydney by a hundred kilometers. I packed my navy cotton swing dress from Britches (a piece of clothing my mother considers *divine,* since it *covers-all touches-nothing*), but now that I see the trailers spread out in front of me, I realize I'll be in Booker's Roanoke lacrosse shorts the whole weekend.

We drive in past the barbecue area, and John gives some folks a neighborly wave. The double-wide is mostly yellow and white inside. There's a tiny sink and a plastic fridge like the one Tracy and I used in college to chill our Milwaukee's Best. Above the kitchenette is a compartment with a mattress where John tosses his bag. The kids take a tiny room with bunk beds, and I apparently have the sofa, which opens into a bed.

"There's a privacy screen on tracks," John says, showing me how to cordon myself off when the time comes.

The kids are eager to get to the beach. Milly stuffs her shovels, rakes, and molds into a mesh bag. Martin dons his sun hat; two flaps bounce around off the back like rubber splash guards on truck tires.

"I can stay and sort out dinner," I offer, assuming John would like some time with the kids.

"No, come along," he says.

"Oh, okay."

I scoop up the inflatable floaties, and we head out single file, through the caravan park and onto a sand path.

"Can we go round to the jetty?" Martin asks, popping a raisin in his mouth.

"Great idea. Just a five-minute walk, Kelly," John says, throwing me with uncharacteristic eye contact.

"There's pelicans!" Martin tells me.

"Pel-i-cans," I say like Captain Kangaroo, "their beaks hold more than their bellies can!"

Martin likes that one.

"And farther round a bit, there's a lookout," Milly adds.

"We used to come here quite a lot," John says, explaining their expertise.

"Tell her about the surfers," Martin prompts.

"The girl surfers," Milly amends.

John explains, "When we first started coming, there were only blokes. But then, over the years, we started to notice some sheilas out there."

"And Mummy said, *Girls can do anything boys can do.*"

"That's right," John and I say at the same time. I look down, embarrassed to have been caught moralizing to the kids when their father is right here and able to do it himself. "They absolutely can," John finishes.

When we get to the end of the path and the ocean opens up before us, Milly draws John to the waterline, and Martin asks me if I know that "twenty-eight percent of the ocean is abyssing."

"I heard something like that. I think it might even be eighty-two percent—"

"That's right! Eighty-two percent!" Martin runs toward the water, turning back to see where I am. "Come, Keely!"

"Yes, come," John insists. The three of them stand in a row, alone on their special beach, waiting for me. "We'll show you the kite-flying stretch."

Now they need me. Now I'm useful.

I'm not here to make bad sandwiches, to paint their nails or heal their chapped lips. That doesn't matter. They need someone to listen to the story of Before—how good it was to swim with Mummy, to bike and collect shells, to jump in the water holding hands off that platform right there. That's what I can do. I can justify the reminiscing. I can take them in, learn their history, witness their suffering and their slow but indisputable survival.

The beach is part of my mother's narrative, too. Her friend Betty Moran had a house on Thirty-fourth Street in Avalon. The Pigeons took over for a week every summer. I tagged along because Mrs. Moran's daughter, Poopsie, and I kept each other occupied making drip castles and playing under the deck with frogs that we'd name and marry off. As we got older, we listened to eight-track tapes and did dance routines for the ladies, with tennis balls stuffed in the tops of our bathing suits.

By the time we became teenagers, Poopsie and I had stopped doing shows and spent the week shadowing our mothers, setting up beach chairs, covering ourselves in Bain de Soleil, playing backgammon. We followed the ladies as they came in from the beach, dragging their monogrammed towels and L.L. Bean totes, showering outside and changing into bright Lilly Pulitzer skirts. The ladies made short drinks with cracked ice and curls of lemon hanging off the rims, and under every glass was a cocktail napkin that said MONEY ISN'T EVERYTHING, BUT IT SURE KEEPS THE KIDS IN TOUCH. Everyone smoked and played cards. Poopsie and I drank grape Fantas, and nobody asked us how many we'd had or told us to slow down.

My mom loved playing gin and could win all night. No one could beat her except Mrs. Maroney, who, I learned that summer, used to go on dates with my dad. "A hundred years ago," Mrs. Maroney said. "Another lifetime."

My mom put her arms on Mrs. Maroney's shoulders and said to me, "How would you like this crazy gal right here to be your mother?" and everyone laughed. Mrs. M. was jokey and she bought me an ice cream once, but even so, I didn't think I was supposed to be some other lady's daughter, and it threw me that my dad had liked someone else before he liked my mom.

"Come over to me, Nelly Norrigan!" Mrs. Wilson said. She lived on our street and had a Swedish accent and liked to pinch my ear. Her first name was Birgitta, but all the Pigeons called her BiBi. She pulled me into her in a way that made me feel special. "What do you think about all this, little Nelly Norrigan?" I told her I thought it was time for me to take her on in backgammon and she said, "*Ooh la la*, little girlie feeling brave."

We set up the board. My mom came over, and I played like she'd taught me. I rolled my dice with the cup, I did the lover's leap, I made points in my home base. But soon enough my mom drifted off to play cards on the screened-in porch, and as her shadow pulled away from the board, I rolled something crappy and panicked.

"Ooh, playing it safe, Nelly Norrigan."

I should have taken a risk, left a man open. I knew it was dumb, but my mom leaving before I was finished flustered me. I wanted her to stand by, be my witness.

A few mornings later, back at Lewiston, I roll over and pull the clock closer so I can read it. Seven-thirty. Shit. I hustle into the kitchen, cleaning my glasses on the shirt I slept in.

"Morning, Kelly," John says.

"Hi. Can I help with lunches?"

"Ta." John is finally letting me take something over.

"Hi, Kelly," Evan says, appearing behind me. It's strange to see him at this hour. Maybe he couldn't sleep. "Morning, John."

John turns to face his stepson. "Good morning, Evan."

"I checked on Pop," Evan reports, as if this is standard family procedure. "He's up. In his chair."

"I'll look in on him," John says. "Thanks."

Evan glances at me on his way out of the kitchen, not touching the morning paper and offering no explanation for his untimely appearance.

While I finish the lunches, John goes outside to cut some blooms from the bushes out front. He brings in a large bouquet, hydrangea, I think, and ties it together with string.

Later, with the kids at school and John painting, I wait for Evan to come in for *Santa Barbara,* but he never does. For lack of anything better to do, I rearrange the cookbooks, balancing the skinny, tall spines with the squatter ones. I wipe down the windowsills and get going on the silverware drawer, removing all the knives, forks, and spoons to clean out their plastic beds. The drawer itself, inside and out, needs attention, which means all the drawers in the kitchen do, which in turn implicates the walls, the baseboards, the whole room. Rehabilitation is addictive. I bet this is why John paints all the time, drawn to work that carries the promise of daily progress and inevitable completion, living for the day he can stand back with his hands on his hips and say, "Our house was shabby and unkempt, and now look, it's shipshape!"

Eventually, after reorganizing the pantry and wiping down each shelf with cleaner, I decide to make Toll House cookies. I have less than an hour before pickup, and I'd rather the house smell like a bakery than a hospital.

While the last batch bakes, I change my shirt, redo my ponytail, and rub some extra deodorant in my pits. There's nothing happening with Mr. Graham, or apparently Evan either, but still, I have my pride.

"Okay, I'm heading out!" I call to John while I set the cookie tray on an extra oven mitt.

"No, no, I got it," he says, stepping into the kitchen with a fresh shirt on and his hair combed, reminding me of the day I met him.

"I thought I'd get them so you could keep painting."

"No more painting. Today, uh, today is Ellen's birthday, so the kids and I are going to take her flowers."

"Oh." I stand upright.

"Martin wants to give her his pinwheel."

"Of course. I'll be here then."

After John leaves, I lower myself into a chair and find that

I've bowed my head and crossed my hands the way I used to in church after taking Communion. I picture Martin piercing the ground with his plastic pinwheel and Milly tilting a bouquet against her mother's headstone. The words *Dear God* come to mind. That's how I started all my petitions growing up, *Dear God,* like I was writing a letter from Camp Tockwogh. Nothing else comes to me after that, so I just say it again. *Dear God. Dear God.* I cover my mouth, looking over my knuckles, my eyes landing on a framed photo of the kids, determined not to cry, because who the hell am I to be crying? I don't know anything. My mom is fine, right where I left her, waiting for me to come home and grow up, or come home grown up.

When the kids and John get back, I look them over for signs of grief—ruddy eyes, grass stains on their knees—but they seem the same.

"That was all right," John says, sounding pleased.

"I'm so glad," I say, happy that he's happy, or happy-ish.

After dinner, John tells the kids they can sleep with him tonight, and as they dash to their room to get in pajamas, he leans back against the counter. "I think it really went well."

I stop the faucet. "I'm so glad," I repeat.

"Yeah," he says, looking at the event from a distance, like a foreman surveying his construction project.

For a moment we stand there, still strangers, but friendly strangers, strangers who can share space, strangers who care, until the kids appear in the doorway ready for Daddy. Now that I understand what today is, I want to find Evan and make sure he knows that somebody is worrying over him, but he never comes in, and I suspect he's working overtime at the store, stocking shelves and breaking down boxes like a madman, trying to hear the sound of his mother's voice saying something perfect, something like *I see you working so hard, honey,* something like *I'm here, I promise.*

As a treat after yesterday's trip to the cemetery, I decide to take the kids straight from school to Darling Harbour to go paddle-boating.

The rental hut is easy to find, and after a short wait, a girl around my age whose name tag says MEGGIE hands us three life preservers and points us toward a row of colorful plastic boats.

"Righto, then, have yourselves a go."

The American in me, conditioned by a thousand TV ads for personal injury lawyers, wants paperwork to sign, a deposit, critical instructions about where not to go. "Go on now," carefree Meggie says to us.

"Ta," I say, and the kids look at me like I'm a total sham. "What? Can't I say *ta*? Ta, luv! Ta, darling! Good on ya. No worries, mates."

"That's not how we talk!" Milly shouts.

"Ah, my little sheila, that's a bit dodgy, now, isn't it?"

"You sound like a pirate!" she says, squinting at me.

"Arrr—"

Martin runs to the boats. "Let's do this one!"

"I'm going in the back," Milly says, carefully climbing on.

Martin's next to me, a yellow life vest hanging loosely off his shoulders.

This is the kind of mother I'm going to be. The kind who gets up and goes, does funny voices, who lives a tourist's life in her hometown, sifting through the paper looking for outings and activities, festivals and nature walks and community potlucks, inspiring her children with her endlessly redoubling energy!

I pedal madly, propelling us by inches. Martin slides forward to help but his feet barely touch the pedals. I sit up straighter to get some leverage. We ride awhile in silence, picking up a nice current. The harbor is huge in front of us. I hope they'll remember this. I should've brought my camera.

After a while, Milly asks, "When do we turn back?"

"Never!" I reprise my pirate voice.

As we get farther out, the water gets choppier. My thighs are burning, but I don't mind, because this is what I'm here to do: wake them up, thrill them, snap them back into their childhoods.

"This is far!" Martin says, glancing back at the dock, which is small now.

I squeeze his knee. "Not far enough! We're going to the ends of the earth, laddie!" I paddle faster and harder. Little waves splash in around our feet.

"When do we go back?" Milly asks.

"We have loads of time!" I paddle on. "We have the boat for an hour. Look out there—see those guys!" I point to a family way out in front of us.

"That's really far," Martin says.

There's a moment of quiet.

"Should we sing a sailing song?" I suggest.

No response.

"Come on, mates, sing something for me to paddle to."

"I want to go back!" Milly shouts. I turn. She has the fire of the betrayed in her eyes. "I want to go home! Now!"

"Oh, honey, we can turn around. Watch this. I can turn us

right around, and we can go back." She is not satisfied. She starts to cry. "Look, there's the docking area. We'll be there in a few minutes."

She cries louder, her usual stoicism falling off like a costume that never really fit.

"We'll get there! Look how fast I'm going," I say desperately. "As fast as I can paddle." She cries bigger still, bigger than she is, as big as machine-gun blasts.

"I can paddle, too!" Martin says, wanting to help.

As I light my thighs on fire paddling us to shore, I think, *Thank God her mother can't see this*. It'd be torture to watch someone mistake your daughter's autonomy routine for actual fearlessness.

That night at bedtime, Martin begs me to read him a section from Milly's *Seven Wonders* book. "Please, just a little?"

I slip into bed next to him and start reading about the Pyramids in a quiet monotone, so Milly will know I remember that the book has bad associations for her. "'The Pyramids were made by thousands of slaves.'"

"What are slaves?"

"Um, people who work but don't get paid. People who have to do whatever the boss tells them to do. They have no choice."

"Like you," Martin says.

"No," I laugh. "I get paid, and I have a choice. I can say no. I can quit."

"You get paid?"

"Of course she does!" Milly calls out from her bed around the corner.

"I do."

"Who pays for you?"

"Daddy does," Milly answers.

"Your dad pays me to help out, to clean up, to drive—"

"You can quit?" Martin asks.

"I *can*. I could. If I needed to. If things were unfair or something."

"Is this fair?" he asks, referring to all of it, I suppose.

"For her!" Milly chimes in.

"Everything's going great." He checks my expression for signs of deceit. "We're good, I promise." With the matter more or less resolved, he turns back around. I squeeze him, wondering when to remind him that, fair or no, even if I wouldn't mind staying a little longer, I still have to leave in early July.

As we move into the "Statue of Zeus" section, Milly sighs like a librarian who's told us to hush once already.

"'Zeus—,'" I start.

Milly throws off her comforter, and for a moment I think she's going to storm out of the room and peel around the house, looking for someone to petition. *Daddy! Pop! Ev! They're reading the stupid boy book and I can't sleep!* But her father is working an overnight flight, her grandfather is too old to be awake after 7:30 P.M., and her half brother is at the supermarket.

Martin elbows me to keep going.

"One sec, bud."

Milly comes around to Martin's bed, her ponytail almost shot, her hair falling around her face the way it does, implying her future self.

"Hi," I say, projecting nonchalance.

She stands at the side of the bed, her eyes on an illustration of Zeus. "When is Daddy coming home?"

"Not until tomorrow." I lift the blanket. "Wanna get in? I

was just going to read one more section—" She looks around, biting her lip. She stares at us, hating her lack of options.

"Fine," she says, and wriggles between my legs, toboggan-style. I'm barely breathing as she rests her head on my chest. "Go," she says.

"'Artemis was the daughter of Zeus,'" I read, stunned, gratified. "'Artemis assisted her mother in the birth of her little brother.'"

"That's revolting," Milly says, making me laugh by choosing the most regal adjective available. "I felt that!" she says. "I felt your laugh." She scrunches down so her head is lower on my stomach, her arms resting on my thighs like I'm a chaise longue.

I take a drink of water.

"Whoa. I heard that. I heard your swallow."

"Me next!" Martin squeals.

Milly turns her head around and looks up at me seriously. "You know the one thing you don't have in common with the emu?"

"The one thing? What is the one thing I do not have in common with the emu?"

"Your Adam's apple doesn't stick out."

"Right," I say. "Because I'm a girl. Only boys have Adam's apples."

"And snakes. Snakes have Adam's apples. I've seen pictures. They have a big bump right here." Milly touches her throat.

"I don't think that's an Adam's apple. Adam's apples have something to do with your voice and your vocal cords, and, you know, snakes don't talk. That big bump is probably a rat or a mouse—"

"Eww," they both say.

"*Eww* is right. They swallow stuff whole."

"Why don't snakes chew?"

"They don't have enough teeth?" I venture. "I'm not sure. I don't know a lot about snakes. Maybe Evan knows—"

"He has a *massive* Adam's apple," Martin announces, his emphasis on *massive* making "Adam's apple" seem like a euphemism.

"Oh, really?" I ask, chuckling.

"I felt you laugh," Milly says. "Do it again."

"Make me laugh again."

"How?"

"Tell me more about Evan's *massive Adam's apple*."

I don't know what happened tonight. I don't know if Milly regrets falling apart on the paddleboat or if this break-and-mend routine is the best she can do, but she came over to Martin's bed. She let me hold her. I can still feel her weight against my chest, and it makes me impatient to be a mother.

After three months of soap operas, at least thirty crosswords, two dinners, and half a game of chess, Evan finally asks me to do something off-campus. He wants to show me the Three Sisters, "a brilliant rock formation" in the Blue Mountains.

"Sounds great. I'll get a roll of film."

"My mate Thomas is coming, if you want to bring your friend Tracy."

"Sure." Is this some sort of double date?

On Saturday morning, Tracy and I hustle out to the driveway in our Reebok aerobic shoes to meet Thomas, who is leaning against his Corolla. He's tall and lean, his pants cinched by a belt clipped on its tightest hole. There's thick white sunblock under his eyes and his teeth are begging for orthodontia. This is not a double date.

After an hour-and-a-half drive, we arrive at the head of the Prince Henry trail and set out single file. "This is a proper bush-walk," Evan says. He moves with authority here, spinning around to point out various *flora* and *fauna,* terms he uses without irony. The Great Outdoors is clearly his psychic home.

Forty-five minutes later, we can no longer see Evan and Thomas on the turns or hear their voices in front of us, but we don't care. We just keep gabbing about how out of shape we are and how we need to do sit-ups and leg lifts every day, or at least three times a week, and then walk two miles on the weekend mornings, or at least one mile at a fast pace. We've had this conversation many times, but we don't acknowledge that as we make our serious plans for This Time. After we exhaust the topic of Diet & Exercise, we flip to another section of the women's magazine that is our lives: Relationships.

We analyze the couple Tracy works for—their marriage and how tired they always seem, except when they get the grog going, and then they are red-cheeked and jolly and seem to like each other much more. Neither of us is going to be like that when we get married. No way. We're going to slow-dance in the kitchen and make out on the sofa. We're going to be in love, even doing dishes, even in the middle of the day, and stay in love! Not like her parents, who divorced, and not like my parents, who are basically like an older sister and her wacky kid brother.

Tracy checks her watch. We've been walking for two hours in one direction, so she thinks maybe we're not doing a loop, as suspected, but rather going up and back, which seems deranged. Who seriously walks for four hours?

We trudge on. Finally, around hour three, we see Evan and Thomas sitting on a bald patch above the trail, eating hunks of ham off the tips of their pocketknives.

"Great, huh?" Evan calls down to us, referring to the valley behind us, which is preposterously lush.

"Beautiful," I say.

"You see the koalas back there?" Thomas asks.

"And potoroos?" Evan adds.

"No, neither," we say together as we climb up the hill and sit down to snack on what doesn't seem like nearly enough food, pretending we're not *totally knackered* and dreaming of helicopter pickups.

"Is this a loop?" I ask hopefully.

Evan shakes his head. "No . . . when we're ready, we just turn around and take the same trail back."

Oh.

I'm ready.

"Cool."

"Whenever," Tracy says, making eyes at me.

As we sit, definitely longer than Thomas and Evan need to, a snippet of conversation floats up from the trail below us.

"Is that an American?" Tracy asks, tilting her head.

I listen with a rising thrill, like a raffle official is calling numbers and my ticket is a one-for-one match. "That is two Americans!" I work myself up to my feet. "Did he just say *lacrosse*?"

A couple of guys reach the clearing below.

"Hey, hi! Are you talking about lacrosse?" I call down, startling them.

"Oh, hello up there. Yeah, we were."

Tracy and I shuffle down the hill, my muscles already bundling, to introduce ourselves.

"I'm Walker, and this is Trey."

Evan and Thomas stand and wave.

I tell them my dad played at the University of Maryland and, after college, brought a team to Australia for an exhibition tour. They think this is very cool, and I knew they would, which is why I led with it. Then the four of us dig around for every sliver of common ground. University of Virginia, Richmond Spiders, Baltimore. We talk faster and louder as we connect, each point of contact like a shot of espresso.

Evan, who looks small next to Walker, is ready to get moving again. None of this means jack to him. But I am so full of the sounds of home, my brothers, my dad, that I can't bear to walk away, so I stretch it out, drinking in a little more Americanness until Walker tells us he's having a party next weekend and we should come.

Of course we should!

"You, too!" he says to Evan and Thomas.

"Thanks, mate," Evan says.

We're all in.

Tracy and I move twice as fast on the way back, caffeinated by the brush with home. On the ride home to Lewiston, I stare at the back of Evan's head, his ponytail, his boots on the dash, cross-examining my interest in him.

Do I like him—like him or is he just the only boy in reach, like the guy at the office who seems like The One during the off-site Lotus 1-2-3 training, but then, when you bump into him over the weekend, with his conscientious friend, safe car, and ham slabs, you wonder what the shit you were thinking? Am I so ravenous I mistook a cracker for a banquet?

The day before the American's party, the kids and I hit the park.

Martin attacks the swings while Milly and some girl dash around collecting things to organize: leaves, tiny flowers, pebbles. It's distinctly satisfying to see them play, like watching dogs hurtle across a beach.

In my book, Ántonia is growing up, wearing heels, trailing a pack of girls to the dancing tents that pop up outside town. Her English is excellent; she can read and write and talk to anyone about anything. She's well known and well liked. But for all her years in America, she is becoming more bohemian, not less. She cooks her mother's recipes, prefers the old music, doesn't seriously consider American suitors. Even if she never again feels her native soil push up between her toes, her emotional return to her country is inevitable. People don't separate from the motherland. Not really.

After an hour, Martin flops over my knees, communicating his total exhaustion. I'm good to go.

"Milly!" I call, lifting a hand to flag her down. She's arranging a dozen leaves from largest to smallest. "Come on! Time to go!"

She doesn't hear me, or doesn't want to.

"Milly!"

Nothing.

"Amelia Tanner, let's get a move on! Time to go!"

Milly's new friend points over at me. "Amelia, your mum's calling you."

Milly's head jerks up. I expect her to recoil at the girl's egregious error, or burst into tears, but she does neither. She smiles and says, "Thanks," and runs right for me, letting the fiction stand.

We can barely look at each other when she reaches us, but for effect, I put my hands on her shoulders. "You hungry? Your brother tells me he is STARVING."

"Yeah, for sure."

If she wants to let some girl think I'm her mother, I say, *Go right ahead*. Her motherlessness need not figure into every interaction, at least not ostensibly. And anyway, kids do this all the time, even kids whose mothers are alive. The first time I pretended someone else was my mother was on Halloween night in sixth grade.

Allison, Barb, and I were going as Snap, Crackle, and Pop in costumes made for us by Allison's mom, who loved to sew. She didn't use patterns or need directions. She made it up as she went along, a Rice Krispies box her only guide.

I was Snap, so I got the striped hat and the white kerchief tied roundly at my neck. Allison's mom rubbed red lipstick in circles on our cheeks and pinned our hats into our hair. She tied and re-tied the sashes at our waists until we looked exactly like the cartoons in the commercials. Then she took our pictures—together, separately—until every flash on her cube was shot. She even made us matching candy bags with the leftover fabric. I held up the pillowcase my mom had given me, and we all laughed.

While she was showing us the outfit she made for Allison's sister, the doorbell rang.

"Oh, girls, I bet that's a trick-or-treater!"

"I'll get it," I volunteered.

When I got downstairs and opened the door, a deliveryman held out an overnight box. "Can you give this to your mom?"

I hesitated, only for a moment, and then accepted the package. "Sure."

"Great costume."

"Thanks!" I said, riding a wave of pride. "My mom made it—from scratch!"

I closed the door and headed back upstairs, relieved that Allison hadn't overheard me owning her mom. I didn't know what I would have said if she had. I wouldn't have told the truth, that's for sure. I wouldn't have said I wanted to pretend I had a different mom, a zippy mom, the kind who worked all week on my Halloween costume, who set aside a whole day to help me become someone adorable and snappy, who used up all her expensive flashbulbs on me and my friends, instead of a relentless pragmatist who gave me a ratty pillowcase to hold my treats along with a warning about how long I would be grounded if I wasn't *in this house by nine P.M. and not one minute later.*

Big party tonight at the American's. I wish we'd run into him earlier. We only have a few more weeks before we leave for the Great Barrier Reef.

While I dry my hair, Tracy reads aloud from the morning paper about Bill Clinton's mythical childhood. A penniless have-not who never met his dad and grew up in a rural ghetto that's actually called Hope.

"People are gonna eat that up. He's everything we like to think is possible in America," I say.

"So here's a line for you." Tracy reads a sidebar about Ross Perot. "'If you see a snake, you kill it. You don't appoint a committee on snakes.'"

"Sounds like something my mom would say."

"Totally. What happened to your bangs?" Tracy asks.

"I torched them. The hair dryer here is total crap. John bought it before I moved in, which was so nice, but this"—I point at my scorched fringe—"is the best I can do, even with my new styling brush that cost like twenty bucks." *Oh for God's sake, Kelly, who's looking at you?* I hear my mother ask.

"Put a little water on your bangs. I can smell the burn."

On the train to the party, Tracy hands me her Zinc Pink, and I coat my lips.

Evan meets us at the station downtown. We glance at each

other, sheepish about our party looks, me in mascara and lipstick, Evan in shoes and a belt. We make small talk as we follow Walker's directions. When we get to the door, Tracy and Evan look to me to do the knocking. Standing in the hallway between them, I don't know who we are or who I want us to be: three pals . . . a couple and their single buddy . . . best friends and some guy?

Walker throws open the door. "You made it!" he says to us, kissing both Tracy and me on the cheek and throwing out his hand for Evan to shake. "Good to see you, mate." He says he thought we might not come, but we'll be glad we did because this party is *going off*. He points Evan toward a keg and takes Tracy and me to the kitchen, where we drain a bottle of wine into giant orange stadium cups that Walker wants us to notice are from UVA.

"Hey," Walker says to the guys in the kitchen, "these are the American girls I told you about." We all shake hands, and everyone is happy to meet us. I glance across at Evan, who is filling his cup, and wonder if he'll surprise me by getting hammered.

"Right, then, American Girl," says an Aussie named Ian. "How do you like 'Stralia?"

I tell Ian I love his country, I can't think of one thing wrong with his country, his country is like a giant resort—gorgeous and open late and geared toward adventure.

"I reckon nothing's better than the States. Fan-bloody-tastic." Ian takes the uncomplicated view of us. Half the people we meet think like Cultural Chernobyl Goatee Boy, and the other half see the United States as Xanadu. It's nice being around that half, nice like when my old friend tells me that my mom's the rudder.

Ian and I talk about nannying, and I keep it simple. I don't tell him the Tanners' sad story. It's a party. We laugh about how hopeless I am, driving on the wrong side of the road, freaking Milly out in Darling Harbour, and then he says he's been on the dole since he got out of uni. *Talk about hopeless,* I hear my mother say.

After an hour, someone puts on Depeche Mode and people start bobbing their heads and tapping their feet. Evan is across the room, talking seriously to a plain girl with very good posture. She suits him. Like Evan (and Milly and my mom), she hails from the part of the world where people are not looking to be noticed. It's a place I haven't chosen to spend much time.

Tracy taps me on the shoulder. "Cig?"

We duck outside and meet a new crowd, the smokers. Someone holds out an open pack, and we each take one and say, "Cheers," like we're locals. I'm glad Evan's not out here; it's insensitive to smoke in front of a person whose family was destroyed by cancer, even if it wasn't lung cancer.

We end up staying outside a long time because Walker's turned up to regale us all with adventure stories. He's done everything—white-water canoeing, wind-surfing, zip-lining, hiking something called the Tarkine Rainforest Track in Tasmania. Walker is totally fearless, a Go For It guy. As he talks, Tracy and I make mental notes of the awesome things we need to do and the off-the-beaten-track places we need to hit.

Eventually, Evan leans out the door, reminding me that in some ways I'm already way off the beaten track.

"Oh, hey," he says to me.

"Hey." I move the ashtray and slide over so he has a place to be. His beer is almost full, and I wonder if he's still on his first.

Folding Evan into his audience, Walker starts a new story, about parasailing. Someone interrupts and asks when he managed to do "all this incredible shit," and he says, "Pretty much over the last year."

"Dude, that's a killer year," someone says.

"Just trying to keep moving and see it all," Walker says. "The best was black-water rafting in New Zealand. Incredible."

Someone asks what *black-water* means.

"Rafting through caves—subterranean." Someone whistles *woo-ee.* "Yeah. Never seen anything like it. The really rad thing is that once you get deep down in the tunnels, there are, like, thousands of glowworms clinging to the walls."

I'd have gone for Walker if I'd met him last year at happy hour on Water Street in Baltimore. Me in my rayon skirt and pleather pumps, him in his JoS. A. Bank suit and genuine leather briefcase, telling me how he's going to be an expat in Australia. Shit, I almost fell for him here, settling in at his feet as he rolled out his director's cut of ripping yarns.

But then Evan came outside and stood next to me, and as I looked back and forth between him and Walker, thinking about what they've each seen and conquered these past twelve months, Walker started to look designed, like a fitness fanatic whose muscles have been carefully shaped in the gym, an expensive trainer guiding his every rep, where Evan is a foot soldier, made fit by a tour of service, no spotters, no mirrors. He's done the night watch, carried a body, guided his unit back to civilian life.

What good is the stuff flashy Walker knows? *Keep moving. See it all.* Why? For the stories? How do they help anybody?

If I have only so much time to learn, I'm pulling my chair up to Evan and begging him to talk. His parents' separation and divorce, his mum's second marriage, her tumor, the treatment and side effects, the first time a doctor used the word *terminal,* deciding how to spend the time left, the first skipped dose, the mess of a body breaking down, the last words, the closing of her eyes, the relief, the fury, the hole. I need to know the things he knows. Everyone does.

Evan is a Person of Great Interest, of True Interest. My mother would have preferred him over Walker from *word one*.

On the ride home, I open the window because I smell like an ashtray, and I stare out at the yellow line marking the road's shoulder until it blurs, mad at myself for ogling over Walker's well-stamped passport and daredevil badges.

You think rafting through the dark is so gutsy, Walker, in your helmet and life preserver?

Try watching your mother die. Try looking after her father and her kids. Try family life.

The next day is gorgeous. Bright but not hot. Outside on a chair, a thin blanket across my thighs, I crack open my book, thinking about my mother and the many moments of my childhood when she tucked herself away somewhere, enjoying what she called *a party for one*.

In the early spring and later fall, when the air was chilly but the sun was warm, she'd settle into a chaise longue she'd set up in a patch of sunlight just inside the garage to read one of her giant library books with the crinkly plastic covers. She loved having a little color in her cheeks and she could not hear the phone out there—or, better yet, us kids.

In the humidity of summer, she could be found sitting in the driveway in her station wagon, enjoying the air-conditioning, opening the mail or making a store list while listening to *MacNeil/Lehrer*.

In the winter, when the sun went down early, she'd slip up to her room, unhook her bra, and lie down on top of her well-made bed. Curled up on her side, hands tucked between her knees, she'd keep her eyes open toward the door, like a doll with a dead battery, until one of us barged in with a grievance of some sort. "Mom! Didn't you hear me calling you? Booker broke my hairband!"

This is the first time, here in Australia, that my life has looked and sounded and moved like hers, from bed to kitchen to car and back, and consequently she is everywhere, like a movie playing across the walls and furniture from hidden projectors.

In my book, Ántonia and Jim have lost touch. He's gone East to "be educated," and she's started a family with a man named Cuzak, also an immigrant. They have a large orchard and many children to work it. The last time Jim saw her, twenty years back, he told Ántonia that there was a time when he would have liked to have had her for "a sweetheart, or a wife, or my mother or my sister, anything that a woman can be to a man."

I put down the book and close my eyes, thinking about Jim's affection for Ántonia, how he wanted to be someone important to her and how much bigger and more lovely that is than simple infatuation.

"Kelly?" I hold my hand up to block the sun. Evan is standing in front of me.

"Oh hi," I say, blinking, not knowing how long I've been asleep.

"Sorry to wake you, but you're getting pretty red." My blanket's on the ground, and I can feel the heat of the sun in my legs. "Maybe you should move your chair back into the shade?" He doesn't want me to get too much sun. He wants me to be careful.

"Oh, right, thanks."

"I'm going to head downtown . . . You need anything?"

"Um, no, I don't think so. Thanks. Tracy and I are going in on Friday."

"Right, then. G'day."

I watch him walk down the driveway, rubbing my eyes, realizing the true nature of my interest in Evan. Like Jim's broad hopes for Ántonia, I want to be someone to Evan, someone useful and good, someone important.

I remember a lecture from one of my lit classes about a theory called "Reader Response," which basically says: More often than not, it's the readers—not the writers—who determine what a book means. The idea is that readers don't come blank to books. Consciously and not, we bring all the biases that come with our nationality, gender, race, class, age. Then you layer onto that the status of our health, employment, relationships, not to mention our particular relationship to each book—who gave it to us, where we read it, what books we've already read— and, as my professor put it, "That massive array of spices has as much to do with the flavor of the soup as whatever the cook intended."

One thing's for sure. There's no telling how *My Ántonia* would taste to me if I had tried it years ago, in class or one summer by the pool, instead of here, a foreigner in a motherless home, spending most of my time with a local boy about my age. And then there's the matter of my mother, who loved it so, and how I seem to be looking for her in every passage.

After Evan is out of sight, I lean back in my chair and survey the yard. Pop has hung a small load of laundry. Through the rows of clothes, I can see the door to Evan's empty room.

I want to go in.

I think I'm going in.

I'm in.

A long, wide shelf bracketed to the wall is covered with gear catalogs, carabiners, rope, an ID card with the lamination peeling off, and about a dozen university textbooks. (Maybe he *is* going back.) The shorts he wears every day are on the floor, along with boxers, socks, hiking boots, and a bandanna. Tossed diagonally across his bare mattress is a down sleeping bag, as if there's no use making up the bed with sheets and pillowcases, since he's just passing through. Pushed against the wall are two twin mattresses, I guess for his brother and sister when they come to visit. On the wall is a sign with the Rovers' line about each individual being the principal agent in his own development. I wonder if part of his enthusiasm for Rovers is a reaction to his mother's death—maybe he's learned it's wise to be prepared, to isolate, and to count only on yourself. Then I wonder if there's anything about the Evan I know—his interests, his pace, his disappearances and appearances, his silences and underreactions, his long hair, his fitness, the attention he gives the kids, how he tinkers with but never fixes his car—that is entirely unrelated to his mother.

Of course, maybe there's nothing about any of us that doesn't in some small way touch back to our mothers. God knows, every day I spend with the Tanners, I feel like I'm opening a tiny flap on one of those advent calendars we used to hang in the kitchen every December 1, except instead of revealing Mary and Joseph and baby Jesus, it's my mother. I can't see all of her yet, but window by window, she is emerging.

John is working the flight to Singapore the day Milly first comes to me to ask for help. Seventeen weeks. That's how long she held out.

"Can you read my story? We have to have someone check it before we turn it in." She's not happy to have to call on me but she has no other options.

"I'd love to," I say, setting aside my journal.

"You write a lot," Milly says.

"You don't have a diary?"

She shakes her head.

"It's fun. I just write down what happens every day." She looks unsatisfied. "So that way, after July, I can remember you. And your crazy brother."

"And Evan."

I smile. I can't help it. "Yes, him, too."

She holds out her paragraph about Tasmania.

Every now and then, when I had a really good paper, I'd ask my mom to read it. I did not ask because I valued her feedback. I asked because I wanted praise, her praise, which was hard to come by. But it never worked. She bypassed artistic merit and centered on everything I considered small-minded and beside the point: spelling, grammar, punctuation. She considered my incisive analysis of *Macbeth*, "Not So Fast, Lady McB!," a massacre of the English language. *What are all these dashes? What's wrong with commas? Why so many parentheticals?*

Milly's Tasmania paper is one sentence with a dozen conjunctions.

"It's excellent!" I lie to Milly, thinking, *How hard was that, Mother?*

"Thank you!"

But I can't help it. "Let's just fix the spelling here." I have to edit her, improve her, and she's not even my kid.

"No," she says, snatching the paper before I can touch my pencil to it. "I like it this way."

"Good. You're right. It's great the way it is."

"Remember Natasha?" she says out of the blue.

"Natasha?"

"The girl—from the park—the one who thought you were my mum?"

"Oh, Natasha. Yes, I do."

"That was so funny when she thought you were my mum. Wasn't it?"

"Yeah—"

"I mean, you and me, we don't even look alike. Do we?"

"You're way prettier."

I wait for her to say something more, but she's busy feeling pretty. As she moves toward the door, she turns and says, "I'm working on a project for you in art."

"Me? Really?"

She nods. "Everyone is making something. Because of Mother's Day."

"Oh," I say, barely able to find my voice. "We can give yours to your dad."

"He won't be here on Friday."

"But he'll be here Sunday."

"The tea is Friday."

"The tea?"

"The tea at school. That's when we give out the presents. You're going to be surprised."

I already am.

That Friday, I go to Milly's classroom. I sit in the back near the door, careful not to block the view of the real mothers.

Mr. Graham welcomes us and explains that the children have been working very hard the last few weeks, thinking about the "special people" who take care of them. I hold Milly's stare.

"We've been talking about all the ways we can show appreciation," Mr. Graham goes on.

"Like not whingeing," a boy in Milly's class says, making all the mothers, and me, chuckle.

"That's right!" Mr. Graham says. "And we're very excited to share our gratitude with a poem. Are we ready?" I'm not. Is Milly? "Okay. Here we go."

"Mothers . . ." says the first girl.

" . . . sing us songs . . ."

" . . . feed us vegetables . . ." Mothers elbow each other and wink at their children as they perform.

" . . . and take us for pizza . . ."

" . . . and treat us to bikkies!" adds the boy who called out *not whingeing,* drawing another big laugh.

"Mothers read to us . . ."

" . . . take us to the park . . ."

" . . . to the movies . . ."

" . . . to the library . . ."

" . . . to dance class . . ." Milly says, unfazed. As I exhale, a few moms turn to me with a nod of appreciation for the situation. We are all impressed with Milly.

It's not until after I put her to bed that night that I can bring myself to think about my mother and the reams of things she did for me that could and should have softened me. What is it about a living mother that makes her so hard to see, to feel, to want, to love, to *like*? What a colossal waste that we can only fully appreciate certain riches—clean clothes, hot showers, good health, mothers—in their absence.

On Sunday morning, I hear John and the kids in the kitchen whispering. An ad on the television says, "This year, make sure Mum knows how much you need her!"

A moment later, the new Milly appears at my door with toast and tea, two homemade cards, and a present wrapped in newspaper. Martin comes in behind her with a picked flower. All the crusty chapping on his lips is gone. I did that.

They sit on the end of my bed, waiting for me to try the toast and sip the tea.

"So good, thank you," I say.

"Read the card," Milly says.

Happy day to Kelly. From Milly. That's all it says. Inside, she's drawn a stick figure waving to me. I open the present. A brown polka-dotted ceramic disk.

"It's a chocolate-chip cookie," she explains.

"Of course it is. Thank you so much. I love it," I say, squeezing her knee. I should get out of bed, but I'm afraid to face John. How can he stand this charade?

"Would you care for some fruit?" Milly asks in a waitressy voice.

"I would love some."

She hops off the bed and heads to the kitchen.

"Are you going to the hospital?" Martin asks me.

"What? No—"

"I don't want to come see you in the hospital."

"You won't have to. I'm not going to the hospital. I'm not sick—"

"But I said to Daddy that next year I was going to make you a vase, and he said you won't be here next year."

"Oh! That's because I have to go home, remember? I can't live here. I have to go to the United States. Where my parents and my brothers live."

"When will you be back?"

"Well, I don't know."

"See!"

"I don't know, because Australia is super far away from America. But I can write you and call you and send you photos and—"

"How will you get home?"

"On an airplane."

"In the sky?"

"Yes, in the sky."

Milly returns with a bowl of pineapple chunks.

Martin reaches for the bowl. "Can I have some?" For Martin, it's pineapple first, Keely's departure second.

"Don't eat Keely's fruit," Milly snaps. "Go in the kitchen if you want some."

He hops up.

"Martin!" I stop him. "Do you know what I'm saying? About going home?"

"Yeah," he says as he rolls out of my room. "You're going in the sky."

What does *going in the sky* mean to Martin? Is that where his father works, his father who is standing in the kitchen in sweatpants and slippers? Or is that where his mother went?

That afternoon, the kids are out back playing and the air inside is muggy with unsaid things, things like *Mother's Day sucks*. John is doing paperwork at the kitchen table. Pop wanders in and out the backdoor with bits of laundry. Evan said he was heading over to his father's house to hang out with his brother and sister, his mysterious other life, but he's still here. I try to get an adult conversation started—there was news about terrible riots in Los Angeles this past week—but no one bites.

Why don't they leave each other? What keeps these men here, pressed up against each other? Surely Pop could find more conversation and activity in a retirement community. Evan could move in with Thomas, drink beers and watch late-night TV and be young. John could pack up the kids and sell this house and start again.

Standing in the hall, adjusting my headphones to get ready for a walk, I catch Evan folding the red wool blanket in the living room and realize that he has not stayed for Pop or the kids. This is not an obligation, the tragic fulfillment of a bedside promise to his mother. He stays because this is where she was. He stays to be near her. These are her things—the sofa that followed her from apartment to first house to second marriage, the photos she chose to keep, her recipes, her blanket. To leave Lewiston is to leave the only place where he might sit for a morning in her favorite spot or smell her scent on a pillow or come across her gardening gloves and secretly slip his hands into them, opening and closing his fists in fantastic synchronicity with her memory.

If my mom died and I couldn't call her up inside myself, I'd pull on a pair of elastic-waistband pants, pour a touch of Smirnoff over ice, and phone a girlfriend to play cards. If that didn't work, I'd try reading a library book on a beach chair, and if that didn't work, I'd take her rosary beads and shake them like a shaman until she came back to me, until I could see her and hear her and feel her again.

By ten A.M., Evan and I are in our chairs, ready for the show. Eden's rapist has yet to be found. Cruz continues to repress his rage publicly, but when no one's around he's crazed, sure it was her doctor.

As the credits roll, I lean back and sigh. "If they don't sort this out before I leave—"

"I'll have to write you with the updates. Did you book your flights?"

"Yeah, next Tuesday." Five nights left, Evan. Tick tock.

He raises his eyebrows like he's just taking this in for the first time, and I nod. For a split second, I think I might lean into him.

"So I was going to tell you, I found my old art portfolio from uni."

"Can I see?"

"Uh, yeah."

"Now?" I nudge.

"I guess so. Okay. Yeah." He stands up, so I do, too. "After you," he says, and I head outside, past the lemon tree, across the driveway, alongside his Scirocco. I stop at the door. We're both nervous.

"Here?" I ask, pretending I don't know where I am.

In his room, he unzips a giant black folder and spreads out

his school drawings on the mattress. A motorcycle, cylinders, city streets. More than some sort of passion or point of view, his work communicates a desire to complete the assignments to his professor's satisfaction. Deeper in the pile are drawings of the human form. A hand, a back and neck, bent over, hair hanging over like a waterfall. No faces. Faces are hard, I bet.

"Do you have anything you did outside of class?" I ask, digging for classified information.

"A few. Not sure where." He doesn't want me in his private portfolio, and maybe that's as it should be. It's not right to drag someone's insides out into the daylight, take a long look, and then walk on, leaving him to dart around scooping up his papers and pictures.

"Oh, actually," he says, surprising me, "I have one drawing." He pulls out a sketch of a bird's nest. His pencil marks are light, the paper undented. It's beautiful and oddly sad.

"This is really good, Evan. You should hang this in the living room."

"John wouldn't want my art in the house."

"Come on."

"I promise you."

I try to say something nice about John, like how he gave Tracy and me a ride downtown last week, but Evan shakes his head and says John recently asked him to start contributing for groceries.

"Did you ever get along?" I ask, and he exhales, the way people do when they're about to say the thing that's been going unsaid.

"We used to do okay. I mean, I can't say it was so obvious to me what Mum saw in him, but I probably wasn't very excited about her dating anyone."

"And then . . ."

"When Mum got sick, he . . . there were so many decisions, and I knew a lot about her situation because I read a lot about tumors and cancer treatments, and my friend's mum is a nurse, so I knew about different options and medications, but he didn't talk to us, me or Pop. He'd come home from the hospital, go in their room, shut the door, and come out with his decision."

I ask why John had all the power.

"He's the husband."

"Right, of course. I was just thinking . . ." I don't know what I was thinking, other than that Evan's life as her son went back twice as far as John's life as her husband, and maybe that should prequalify Evan.

Though if my mother ever has a fatal disease, my brothers and I will have no say whatsoever. For that matter, neither will my father. She will not allow us to be the ones to withhold her medication, turn off her respirator, let her die. As far as she's concerned, those decisions are hers alone, and she's made them, along with every detail of what happens after. At her funeral, someone talented will sing "Ave Maria," the long version. There will be a program, but no photo. Between her birth date and the day she died, there will be an extra long dash, because *Let me tell you something, Kelly, it's what happens in the dash that matters*. She will be cremated, unthinkable as the process is, and the ashes from that fire will be spread in three places: the woods near our swim club, the backyard at Wooded Lane, and the beach off Thirty-fourth Street in Avalon. She will be let go peacefully into the hands of a God who knows her full name and every hair on her head and who will deliver her to the field in heaven— the green, green grass of home—where Libby, TJ, and Slugger wait for her with her brother, Tommy.

I'm tempted to ask Evan if it's possible that his mother made all the decisions and John was just the messenger, but I don't know enough about cancer and what it does to a person to go that far, so I say the feeble, haggard, deeply true thing that everyone says even though it doesn't help at all: "I'm so sorry."

I haven't had a working watch since I went swimming at Bondi a month back in my Anne Klein from Filene's, but I know it's at least one A.M., maybe closer to two.

Tracy and I went out hard. We saw a band called the One Hit Wonders. They brought the house down with "My Sharona" and "Tainted Love" and the best ever, "867-5309." Everybody sang along, and it felt like Friday night at Lambda Chi all over again. I've been thoroughly overserved.

On my way up the driveway, I grab a stick to swat down all the spiderwebs. It's automatic now, as though this is actually the house where I live. For all my swinging and swatting in the dark, I'm still draped in silk threads that I can feel but not see.

John left a light on in the kitchen to guide me. Thoughtful. When I lean in to turn it off, there's Ev, holding a magazine, drinking what smells like coffee. He's so strange and cute and old.

"No work tonight?" I ask, surprised.

"Naw, new schedule."

"Oh, well, hi. Is that coffee?"

"Decaf."

He never goes out and gets ripped and sings "She Blinded Me with Science" arm in arm with a bunch of strangers.

"Just gonna get some water. Stave off the hangover, you know." I enter his space and get a glass.

"Where'd you guys go?"

"Epping Hotel." I lean back on the counter, taking a long drink, standing as close to him as I ever have, made bold by many pints of VB. "You haven't seen my book, have you? I can't find it."

"No, sorry."

"I think I left it on the train the other day."

"Too bad," he says. "All right, well . . ."

"Well . . ."

"I guess I better get some sleep."

"Me, too," I say, pushing myself away from the counter.

In my room, I stand by my bed, rubbing at traces of spiderweb on my neck, mad with frustration and urges. Maybe he doesn't like me—after all this.

Of course he likes me. He tried to teach me to play chess!

Before I can think twice, I'm back in the kitchen.

"Forget something?" he asks.

I look at him and say, "Nope."

And then I stand there, waiting, sure I will ignite if he doesn't come over, if he doesn't take four steps forward. But he does.

He crosses the once-enormous-now-tiny kitchen. He puts his arms around my waist and leans in and kisses me and it is so blood-tingling to finally be kissing him that I can't kiss him enough. I kiss him to make up for every minute we've spent together not kissing. I kiss him like he swam the Nile to get to me, like a prisoner released, like it's his first kiss, like it's his last, like I can bring him back from the dead. *I will do that, Evan, I will kiss you until you feel like yourself again, until you revert to your true age and become just another cheeky bugger—bold, hungry, unstoppable—trying to shag the American girl who's come to care for your half siblings. I will be that girl, Evan. I will lie down—in this kitchen, on this floor, if that's what you want—and let you walk over me like a bridge to the rest of your life.*

Before I get out of bed, I relive last night. Must have been twenty minutes we mauled each other against the refrigerator. Fan-bloody-tastic. The thought of seeing him this morning, however, is so agonizing that I dash to the kitchen for a cup of coffee and slip back into my room without even putting milk in.

A minute later, Martin peeks in my door. I'm going to miss him, his cheer and wide openness.

"Hey, mister," I say.

"What's your name?" The call-and-response is back.

"Kelly."

"What's your mum's name?"

"Mary."

"What's your name?" he starts again.

"What's *your* name?" I take over, wondering if this is what he's wanted all along.

"Martin Tanner!" There's glee in his eyes. He knows what comes next.

"What's *your* mom's name?"

He revs his engine to bust through the barricade. "Mummy!"

"Ellen. Your mom's name is Ellen," I say, picking him up.

"ELLEN!" he repeats triumphantly, like he just filled in the last five squares on a crossword puzzle that everyone else had given up on.

"Ellen Tanner!"

"MUMMY ELLEN TANNER!" he belts out with true ec-stasy. "MUMMY ELLEN TANNER."

"That's right!" It's okay to say it now, I'm sure.

Milly appears at my door, and I'm afraid we'll be repri-manded Captain von Trapp style, but she's distracted by a letter. "Look, Keely! From your mummy. And there's a picture in here. I can see it! I can feel the edges!"

I open the envelope and lift out a snapshot of my family, arm in arm on the lacrosse field at Washington and Lee. "Okay, here we go. Guys," I say, as if I'm actually introducing everyone, "meet my family."

The kids each take an edge of the photo, practically crawling into it, hunching over to pass their eyes across every person's face. Booker in Ray-Bans and flip-flops; GT suited up in his gear with blackout under his eyes. Me in a borrowed red mini-dress that, I see now, does nothing but exaggerate my blocky figure. My dad in Bermuda shorts; my mom in a plaid A-line skirt and Jackie O glasses.

"That's your mum," Milly whispers, as intrigued to see my mother as I was to see hers.

"That's her."

"What's her name?"

"You sound like your bro—"

"It's Mary!" Martin shouts. "Her name is Mary."

"That's right. Mary Dwyer Corrigan."

"You don't look like her," Milly says, surprised.

"No, I don't. I look like my dad, like you look like your dad."

"And my mom, too," she corrects. "I can show you," she says, opening the bottom drawer of a small dresser in my closet and pulling out an envelope of photos that says FREE DOUBLE PRINTS! twice. "See?" she says, handing me a shot of the three of them.

"Wow, you're so right. You do look like her. She's so pretty." Milly smiles and spreads out the photos across my bed.

"You could take one of these," Martin says.

"We have tons of extras."

"I would love that. Which one is a good one?" Milly hands me a shot of her and her brother and her mom, out by the pool. "Thank you so much, Milly," I say, referring to much more than this fuzzy four-by-six.

"You're welcome," she auto-replies, referring, I'm sure, only to the photo.

"I will keep—" The phone rings and both kids pop up to get it, sure "It's Daddy!" and that takes precedence over looking through some old snapshots, even of their mother.

"Hey, before you go, have you guys seen Evan today?"

"He left this morning to help Thomas fix his car," Milly reports on her way to the kitchen, trusting me to tidy up the pictures, slide them in their envelope and back in their drawer so, in case it's ever called into question again, Milly can prove her resemblance to Mummy Ellen Tanner.

That afternoon, I beat it down to the chemist to buy red and purple Rit fabric dye. If I have to live another six months in the same ten pieces of clothing, I can at least change the colors.

First, clean all garments, the instructions say. I know exactly where to go. Standing at Pop's door, I knock gently, and he calls me in.

"Hi. I was wondering if you've started the laundry already?"

He sees the bundle in my arms and beams. "No, I have not. Let's get going, shall we?" He lifts himself slowly, pushing up on the arms of his chair. "That right there looks like a nice load."

I follow him down the hall and hand him my sweatshirt, a turtleneck that my mom sent me after I told her about the cold Sydney mornings, a couple of T-shirts, and a pair of boxer shorts that baffle Pop.

"I sleep in them."

"If you say so."

He pats down the clothes, his face bright with joy and usefulness. He's whistling. I could have kept him busy. I should have.

"Afternoon," Evan says, coming in the side door.

Pop and I both turn. I can feel myself oversmiling. Thank God Pop's here to keep the conversation superficial.

"Hello, Evan. You'll have to wait on your laundry today. Kelly here has a load in the works." Evan and I grin at each other, and I blush, but Pop is so focused on the sounds of the washing machine, no one is the wiser.

"I should be able to get by," Evan says.

"Thanks," I say in a tone that says I'm taking the disruption to the day's workflow very seriously.

"I'm off to the store. Won't be home until late. Kelly, I thought I could take you to the art museum tomorrow if you want, for your last day."

"Oh, sure. Great. Definitely. Yeah." I halt the blathering there.

"All right, then. You two have a good night."

"What's that?" Pop says.

"Going to work."

"Good boy."

He is. He really is.

With Evan working and John out for the night, I ask Pop if he wants to have dinner with me after I get the kids taken care of. He smiles and says he'll bring the wine.

That evening, the kids are angels, one of those lucky nights when everyone gets along, like how your hair always looks extra good the day before you're scheduled to get it cut. Pajamas on, teeth brushed, blankets tucked around bodies, all without a single nag. I leave them in their beds, shining flashlights on their books, and join Pop at the table.

"Can I make you a glass of wine?" Pop offers, holding the tap on a box of Franzia.

"Please."

He fills the glass to the tippy-top, like they do at Red Lobster. I'm tempted to joke that he's trying to get me drunk, but I don't even know if he has a sense of humor, so I just say, "Cheers." He nods and raises his glass carefully.

"I hope the food's okay," I say. "I'm not a big cook."

"It smells marvelous." He's a gentleman from another era.

"It's curry. I found a recipe that was starred, so I thought that must be a good one."

"We loved curry," he says, the *we* referring to I don't know who.

"I think we're about seven minutes away. The rice is still cooking." I bring out our plates, and he winks when he sees that I set the table with the same china Evan used. "So you're from Fiji?"

He explains, in his old-man voice with his old-man pacing, that he grew up in Australia, spent his youth there, but moved over to Fiji after he was married. "She always wanted to come back here, though."

"Your wife?"

"Yes. Have I shown you her photo?" I shake my head. "Well, one moment, then!" He pushes back his chair and rises slowly, shuffling across the hardwood.

I check the rice. The simmering fish is getting too tough to wait any longer. I plate two dinners of chewy rice and hard fish, feeling every bit my mother's daughter.

"Here she is," he says.

I put our plates down. "What a beauty."

"Indeed."

While we work through our dinner, I ask him where the photo was taken, and he tells me about this house and that holiday and how good things were, and I listen, wondering how long it's been since he's said this many words in a row.

After he's told me enough about his Bette, we drift into the population problem, and that leads us to his best mate's widow, a former activist named Dove. He worries about her something terrible. "She's all alone." I tell him he should take her out for lunch, and he laughs and says Ellie used to say the same thing. We talk about the Olympics, cricket, and U.S. football. He can't remember what our big contest is—the Super Cup?—and I say, Close: Super *Bowl*. I tell him how Eugenia Brown fired me. We talk about tennis and hiking in the Blue Mountains and how I almost had to be brought out on a stretcher and I say I really need to do some Jazzercise.

"Ellie used to do that jumping around. She and all the ladies around town," he says, shaking his head, imagining his daughter and her girlfriends grapevining. "She had so many leotards. I must've washed one every day."

"Kept you busy—"

"Kept herself busy is right," he says, not quite hearing me. "Always up to something."

"Did she work?"

"No. Not in a job."

"My mom liked to say she never knew a woman who didn't work *all damn day*," I reply, yoking my mom to his daughter, and not for the first time.

We talk about his recliner; it doesn't work anymore. I tell him my plan to dye my clothes and he says he'll find me a bucket, he thinks they have a tub in the garage, but we keep sliding back to his daughter. He's got another picture to show me. He's going to go get it.

I top off my wine.

What a terrible mistake I've made, leaving Pop in his room to rest himself to death while I sat in this house "alone." He could have been my guide. He would have told me anything, everything. I need to write Libby and Slug more, and visit them as soon as I get home.

"Here it is!" he says from inside his room.

I head in, crossing into his space. "Show me."

He turns his head. "This is Ellen with her mum."

"Look at those two."

"Look at those two is right!" he says, putting his hand on my shoulder.

"Wait. I found a picture of you and Ellen—" I leave him for a moment while I dash into the living room. "Here!" I call. "How about this one?" I hand it to him in the hallway, where we meet.

"Ah, oh, yes." He has tears in his voice. "That's her exactly. That's my girl," he says, using my father's phrasing.

After letting Pop live in that image for another moment, I say, "I hope I've done an all-right job around here."

"I'll tell you one thing. This is the happiest Evan's been in a long time." Old people and their hyper-calibrated radar. They can't hear a word, and they can barely get out of their chairs, but they've got six or seven other senses, scanning, collecting, decoding.

"Oh, wow, okay, that's good."

"Well, dear," he says, looking from his clean plate to his watch, "I'm out past curfew."

"Of course. I'm so glad we did this."

He kisses me on the forehead. "Me, too, dearie."

I go into my room and drop onto the bed and before I know what's happening, I'm crying. I'm crying because up until the other night, I half thought I'd misread the Evan thing, or made it all up, and now I understand that it's been real and palpable the whole time and I made someone happier than he's been *in a long time,* and that feels giant, epic. And I cry because I wish I could have given this family more than I have, something meaningful and lasting, more than just walking with them through Wonderland, the Blue Mountains, the Avoca Caravan Park, more than just letting them show me pictures and tell me stories, something as big and important as what they've given me. I fall back on my bed, thinking about my mom and the things we have and have not been able to give each other, yet, and I hug my pillow like I used to hug hers, the one that smelled just like her, a heady mix of face powder, Final Net, and hand cream.

Big date with Evan today. I'm trying to make myself look decent, but Milly borrowed my good horsehair brush that I spent a day's pay on, and I haven't seen it since. I look through all my stuff, out back near the pool, in the loo.

"Milly—" I call. "Milly, have you seen my hairbrush?" She comes to my door, the picture of anxiety. "I need to dry my hair. See how bad it looks."

"I don't have it."

"Do you know where it might be?"

"No. Why don't you wear your pretty cap?" she suggests, pointing to the sequined elephant hat I bought in Thailand.

"Maybe." While I pull on the madras pants I bought at the Glebe Markets with my newly lavender sweatshirt that matches perfectly, Milly disappears and returns, announcing that she JUST SAW the hairbrush. In my bathroom, of all places. "Where are you going, anyway?"

"Uh, out with Evan. To run errands."

Eventually, Evan shows up wearing his jeans with a button-down shirt you'd buy at a camping store, the fast-drying kind you can wash in a river, and holding three roses.

"Hi, Ev. Doesn't Keely look very special in her purple clothes?" Milly says, making nice.

"She does."

"Hey, Milly, I think Ev brought you flowers," I preempt, looking to Evan apologetically.

"Oh, thank you!" she says in a *Who . . . me?* voice, accepting the tiny bouquet like a Broadway diva.

Evan grins. "You're welcome."

As we head down the street to the train station, Evan says he saw my jeans on the line, and he thinks they turned out well.

"Me, too. I feel like I have a whole new wardrobe. Did you see I turned Pop's skivvies pink?"

"He showed me."

"I felt awful. I rinsed everything in the bucket like ten times before I put it in the dryer. Was he mad?"

Evan laughs. "No. Not after your dinner together."

"Yeah, well, we're dating now."

"Ha! I knew he was moving in."

"So, I finally got a picture from home of my family." I slide it out of my pocket and hand it over. He smiles.

"Classic. You guys are so American," Evan says, referring to some defining feature evident even in this wide-shot photo.

"Really?" We can go as far away as we want—as far as we can get—and an outsider can take one look at us and know our originating longitude and latitude. "Definitely. Look at those choppers: totally American."

"My parents paid a lot of money for those teeth."

He laughs and looks down at the photo again. "I always wondered what it would be like to have a totally normal life— with one family the whole time."

"Oh—"

"No, I mean, it's no big deal. Just, I wonder sometimes. Anyway, this museum is really cool. We can start with the Australian artists."

In the first gallery, we walk through the super-modern work of John Olson, whose paintings look like they were done quickly with loud music playing. "Strings," Evan suggests. The walls are so white, you can hardly make out the ceiling from the floor. Evan stands in the middle of it all, talking more than he ever has. This artist was a rebel, this one was a recluse, this one started a colony that's still active today. Out of the house, on his own terms, with a girl he kissed for a long time in the kitchen, he seems like more than a boy who lost his mom. He seems like a whole person.

After the museum, we make our way to the royal gardens. We don't hold hands, but every so often we brush against each other deliberately, by releasing our balance. We pass seniors on benches and young couples sitting close on blankets in the grass. I'm trying to figure out how to become one of them when Ev says, "I really wish you could meet her," and I snap to, knowing immediately who he means by *her,* feeling her presence like a sudden wind.

"Me, too. I've thought about meeting her." And then I blurt out, "I don't know how you stand it, her being gone."

We walk a few steps in silence before he explains that some times are worse than others. "Like the first time we played chess. And I saw an envelope addressed to your mum."

"I'm so sorry."

"No, no. Don't be sorry. Everyone can't be sorry for having a mum. That's one thing I've sorted out." We go a little farther. "Anyway, I just think you would've liked my mum. And she'd have really liked you."

Although I can stop the tears from running down my face, I can't stop them from filling my eyes, so I look down and so does he, and I'm sorry I don't have the composure to ask him to tell me everything he can remember about his mum for as long as it takes. But I think that's all he needed to say. *She'd have really liked you.*

Over sausage rolls at the cake shop, he retreats from the tender ground of his mother to the nonsense of *Santa Barbara*. We have to wean ourselves, *pathetic the hours we've squandered,* but by the time we're finished eating we decide we're in too deep now, we must find out once and for all who did what to Eden. When Evan says he's 100 percent sure it was the doctor, I can hear his disdain for the whole lot of them. He's like Cruz that way.

As we leave the shop, Evan says, "Those rolls were good—nice and moist," and I grimace.

"You can't say that word. Everyone hates that word."

He laughs so hard. "Any others?"

"I always thought *panties* was kinda creepy. You?"

"Panties?"

"NO! Words you don't like."

"Ah, no. I don't think so. Well . . . brace yourself."

"Hit me."

"No, those are the words I hate. *Brace yourself.* I hate it when people say, *Brace yourself.* It's like, *Why? Because that will make it better?*"

I promise him I will never say that, referring to the future, even though tomorrow this will all be over, and our knowing each other will begin the long slow process of calcification, Evan remembering it his way, me mine—*an American girl who lived with us . . . a boy I once knew*—just like in my book. Jim named his recollections of Ántonia "*My Ántonia*" not to show romantic possession, but because he understood that *his* Ántonia was only one version of her and, at least partially, his creation.

"Let's go to the pub. I'll teach you to play Spit," I say, relaxed by the fact of our futureless situation.

We find an open table at Jackson's, and I pull a deck of cards out of my Thai backpack.

"That's really cool." Evan likes the way I shuffle.

"I've been trying to teach the kids. We played a lot of cards growing up. My mom's a real shark."

"You miss her?" he asks.

"Yeah, I do, a little." It feels good to feel that, and I wonder if I can remember it once my mother and I are in the same country, town, kitchen.

After four pints each, we board the train for Lewiston. Sixty-four ounces of high-alcohol-content lager: That's what it takes for Evan to put his arm around me as the train rattles along. After he steps off the train, he turns around and holds out his hand. I take it, and we don't let go. When we can see the orange porch from a couple of houses away, he stops and kisses me and I kiss him back and we stand on the sidewalk doing that for a long time and it is totally fucking awesome.

Mothers are everywhere. Blame evolution. Or Freud. Or the network executives who can't stop re-creating June Cleaver and the greeting-card executives who can't stop promoting Mother's Day. Blame mother-of-pearl, Mother May I?, or that camp song that starts "Hello Muddah." Blame Disney's stable of step-mothers and godmothers and dead mothers. Blame the Old Lady in the Shoe and her teeming brood or Joan Crawford or Madonna. Blame Mothers Goose and Hubbard, Superior and Teresa. Blame Mr. Mom or the Queen Mum. Blame the metaphor-makers for Mother Tongue, Mother Nature, Mother Lode, Mother Ship, Mother Earth. Pin it on whoever you want, but let me tell you, it's not easy to get from sunup to sundown in this world without bumping up against a mother-something.

Except at the Tanners'. Apart from the other day with Martin and a few short conversations with Evan, here we steer clear of explicit mentions. In fact, I've sidestepped the word at every turn, even avoiding seemingly unrelated topics like kangaroos, because the minute you start talking kangaroos, someone mentions those cute little joeys riding around in mummy's pouch, and *zzt,* you've tripped the wire. So after five months, I know only a touch more about their mother than I did on day one. She made soup from scratch and colored her hair, she had a failed marriage and two sets of children, she did Jazzercise and would have liked me.

Then tonight, my last night, John tells me the kids want to show me a video of their mum, and I almost have to brace myself while waves of relief and gratitude and fear roll through me.

John cues up the tape and announces that the video is ready. The kids race over to the TV area. Ev shares a seat with Milly, and I take Martin on my lap, pulling him close, wanting to memorize him. John stands next to the VCR, emceeing. We look like a family.

"Okay, the camerawork isn't excellent. But here we go," John says, pushing Play.

A title card comes up: EASTWOOD CHURCH PRESENTS THE FIDDLER ON THE ROOF.

The video was shot from a tripod in the main aisle, and the sound is fuzzy. "John was the lead," Evan says earnestly. "Mum was in the chorus." The staging is simple, a rural backdrop, lots of straw, a low roof, a man with a fiddle.

John was an actor? John sang?

"They didn't know each other!" Milly says, eyes forward, tracking the image.

John fixes on the screen while he talks, I think to me. "We met in rehearsals. This was closing night. It ran for two weekends."

The opening number kicks in, "Tradition." Despite his old-man makeup, John looks much younger—hardy and sure—as he and the female lead go back and forth about their duties. He must make a living and study the Torah; she must keep a kosher home and raise the children.

As the chorus steps forward to sing the refrain, Martin hops off my lap. "That's her," he says, pointing to one of many women in burlap head scarves.

"That's not her! That's her!" Milly calls out.

"You're wrong! *That's* Mummy!"

They don't know. Fault the layman camerawork or the generic costumes or too much time passed, but they can't identify their mother. They can't pick her out.

"No, that's Mummy right there!"

"No," Evan and John say at the same time, silencing the piercing squabble. They look at each other, and Evan recedes. This part of her story isn't his to tell, and he seems to know that.

"No, this is Mum, right here—see?" John says, approaching the TV, tapping the screen. "She's right here." The joy of reunion lifts his voice, as if she's really right here, as if he's really touching her.

"I see her! I see her! There she is!" they cry with relief.

So it wasn't in an airport, over a cuppa, in his Qantas blues. He was not pressed and trimmed. He was singing. She fell in love with a man who sang, who danced, who played the doting father, who carried the show.

Before bed, Martin comes to give me a hug. I love him. He tells me he's sleeping with Daddy tonight.

"Before you go, run and snag me some envelopes from the drawer in the kitchen?" I ask.

"For what?" he asks.

"You'll see."

When Martin brings back two envelopes, Milly is behind him. I stamp and address them to Kelly Corrigan, c/o the American Express office in Brisbane, and Kelly Corrigan, c/o the American Express office in Christ Church, New Zealand. "Now all you have to do is put something in the envelopes."

"Like what?" Martin says.

"Like a letter, duh," Milly answers.

"Or drawings or poems or whatever." I tell Martin I want to know everything. We agree to write *every single day*, even though I'm sure he'll forget me in a weekend; I've never seen him worry over people who aren't here. He's present tense, standing in his underwear, holding any hand that's free.

"Tell me about school, about your buddies, all your dinosaurs, trips you take, art you make——"

"Cakes we bakes!"

"Yes, and all visits to lakes. And put in your school photo when you get it."

"I will do that." Martin takes an envelope out of my hand and I hold out the other for Milly. Finally, she takes it.

"All right, guys," John calls from down the hall, "come on, let's get in bed. Kelly needs to get organized!" The kids scurry to his room, and I slip outside to find Evan before he leaves for work.

I cough when I get to the driveway, and he leans his head out of the garage. "Hey."

"Hey. I wanted to say goodbye before tomorrow, when everyone's around."

"Yeah. Me, too. But wait. Hold on." He disappears and is back in a minute. "I got you something——" He hands me a paperback copy of *My Ántonia*. "So you can see how it ends."

"Oh God, how did you know? I can't believe you," I say, taking the book.

We stand close. I want to thank him for keeping me company and teaching me how to play chess and not give up on crosswords, and tell him that my mom would like him so much, but as soon as I start talking, I realize I'm not ready to leave and that I kind of love this person I'm looking at and I'm sure I'll never know anyone else like him because he's cautious and timid and I'm blunt and impatient and we wouldn't make sense in any context other than this one.

I say, "I started to write you a note last night, to make sure I said what I wanted to say, but it sounded stupid. But the thing is, what I really want you to know is that I admire you."

"Me?"

"Yes, you. I mean, not when we first met." He smiles. "When we first met, I thought you were a total soap-opera junkie bum who camped out in a garage." He laughs. "But then it was so obvious that you're not. People need you. You're . . . *important*. You're probably the most important person I've ever met."

"Yeah, right," he sidesteps the compliment.

"No, really. You're the only person I know who's actually doing anything worthwhile: staying here, working nights so you can be around for Pop and the kids. All my college friends have these bogus desk jobs, and look at me, I'm basically planning my existence around a dive trip."

"That'll be one for the books."

This was one for the books, I think. *You* are one for the books.

"Kelly, we'll be out in the car," John calls from the kitchen. It's over. This morning, I leave.

"Be right there." I tuck my toothbrush into my backpack and peek around Pop's door, worried he might not be awake this early.

"Righto!" He looks up from his recliner.

"So, we're heading out," I say, stepping close to him. He takes my hand and nods, smiling. "Thanks a lot for, I don't know, for everything—doing my laundry and eating my bad curry and helping me dye my clothes—"

"Okay, Kelly dear," he says, his eyes shining. "You be safe. Take good care to always be safe."

"I will, I promise. And I'll send you postcards."

"That's nice. That'll be very nice."

"Okay, well—"

"I'll pray for you," he promises.

I lean in and kiss him on the cheek, knowing that I'll never see him again and knowing that, if anything, I should be praying for him.

During the car ride, when I'd planned to ensure that Martin understood I was not going to a hospital, all I can do is look out the window and take long quiet breaths to keep myself from crying. Thankfully, the kids can't see me from the back, and anyway they're busy campaigning for an ice cream stop on the way home, which John thinks they might be able to squeeze in if they get through their errands without any complaining. We drive through St. Leonards to the Pacific Highway. Passing the harbor, I take a last look at the opera house and Circular Quay. By the time we hit the expressway, the morning sun has taken over the sky. I keep wanting to say something, something meaningful that suits the occasion, like how I've realized that things *do* happen in a house. But I never shared my theory with the Tanners, so there's no sense telling them I was wrong, things definitely happen in a house—big, hard, beautiful things. And besides, they already knew that.

John hits the blinker. We're here, the international terminal. Everyone unbuckles. John sets my backpack on the curb. He looks nice, almost rested. "Well, Kelly, thank you."

"Oh, I'm so grateful—thank you for having me."

"Of course. And we can't forget this," he says, handing me my last eighty dollars.

"Right, thanks. I'll put it to good use." We hug for the first and last time.

"You'll be right," he says, like a professor who reveals at the end of a tense semester that he always knew I'd pass.

I lean over and pick up Martin. "I put the T. Rex you loaned me on the kitchen table this morning."

"You could take him."

"He's happy with you. So, you're all set to write me, right, mister?"

"Write, right, right!"

"Good. I'll be watching the mail." I hug him and hug him again. "You are the best boy, the very best boy."

"You are a silly," he says as I smother him.

I pick up Milly. "You're a big girl, lady." I hold out my sequined elephant hat that she said she liked. "So, I thought you could take care of my fancy cap?"

"It's not my size."

"Maybe you could grow into it?"

"But I have my own hat that Daddy got me from Singapore." She doesn't need my wampum. She has the real thing.

"Right." I hug her as long as she'll let me, for my sake, not hers. In the scope of their story, which has so many characters and chapters already, I'm a bit part: *Unnamed girl, American*. I didn't change them or fix them or nudge them gently from one stage of grief to another. That work is theirs to do, and they are doing it.

"Can we take a photo?" I ask, handing John my camera.

"Good idea," he says. Martin crawls back up my side so I have a kid in each arm. "Smile . . ." After the picture, I put them down, feeling like I might buckle with emotion.

"Tell Tracy Tuttle to be a good girl," Martin says.

"I will."

John holds up my pack so I can step in. "All right," he says, untwisting one of my straps, "You have everything? Passport? Ticket?"

"Yup. Thanks."

"Do you have the ceramic cookie I made you in art?" Milly asks, suddenly.

"Of course I do." I pat my backpack. "Wrapped up in a T-shirt so it won't break."

"Good. Mr. Graham said it was the best sculpture I've ever done."

"And I get to keep it," I marvel.

"Of course you do! I made it special for you," she says.

"I love it." I swallow hard.

"Keely, are you going to cry?" Martin says in a consoling, grown-up tone.

"No, now you're the silly."

"Don't be sad," he says, ignoring my deflection. "You have Tracy Tuttle to be with you."

"You're right, I do." I squeeze him one last time and pat Milly's shoulder. "Make your dad stop for ice cream."

"We will!"

John smiles at me. I head toward the giant sliding doors, looking back across the median strip through watery eyes. The kids are happy, waving and leaning into their father. They have a great day ahead. Dropping me off was no big deal. Their perception of painful goodbyes has been recalibrated.

But even if by Christmas Evan has to help them remember the name of their first nanny (*It starts with a K . . .*), I'll always be able to see their faces coming up through the pool's surface, or wrapped in a bath towel, or asleep on the arm of the gold velvet chair in front of the television, and hear the sound of Martin saying *Crustinsashus,* or Milly saying *revolting,* or both of them saying *Keely,* and remember where I was when I opened my first Mother's Day card and learned the one thing I do not have in common with an emu and absorbed the complete lyrics of *Beauty and the Beast.* I'll know it was the Tanner kids who pointed me back toward my own mother, hungry to understand her in a way that I clearly didn't yet. They put her voice in my head. They changed her from a prosaic given to something not everyone has, but of course none of this matters to them. They've got errands to run, and then, maybe, sundaes.

Inside the terminal, Tracy is waiting for me.

"Aw, Kel," she says when she sees my wet cheeks.

"Oh God, those kids," I say as we hug. "Breaks my heart."

"They'll be okay."

"I know. I know." I wipe my face and press my fingertips into my tear ducts to stop myself from bawling. "That was so much more intense than I expected."

"The goodbye?"

"The whole thing."

During the flight, a stewardess named Bronwyn comes to our seats and asks if we are "the Americans, Kelly and Tracy?" We tell her we are, and she says, "Well, then, why don't you follow me?"

As she takes us to the cockpit, she explains that she's a friend of John's and he asked that we be brought up to see the Great Barrier Reef from the air. It's huge, so much bigger than I imagined, giant swooshes of electric blue and green, like an abstract painting or that sand art that people sell in desert towns. Tracy mentions sharks—a Kiwi was recently bitten in shallow waters—but I ignore her worry to ask Bronwyn if John has ever brought Martin and Milly up here.

"For sure."

"Boy, I'd have paid a lot of money to see their reactions."

"You sound like a mother," Tracy teases, and the three of us smile at the absurdity.

Bronwyn says only one of us can stay up here for the landing, which is fine by Tracy, who is ready to go back to the cabin. Safety first.

After I strap into the jump seat, the captain asks who I like in our presidential election, and once we get a conversation going, he slams our policy in Iraq and asks what the riots in L.A. were all about. I'm tempted to roll over. I don't understand much about either topic and I know not everyone loves us. We're too unionized and make bad soap operas and love a liability waiver and generate our fair share of pollution, intellectual and otherwise. But it's my home, and not just because I grew up pledging my allegiance and taking tests on the Electoral College and Pearl Harbor. It's in me, running through me like my mother's blood.

"The thing about the U.S.," I say, "is that it's messy, and complicated, and flawed as hell—but it's also amazing."

"I suppose that's right," the pilot concedes, rewarding my defense of the motherland in a way he'll never appreciate.

As Tracy and I leave, the stewardess hands us a cold bottle of champagne wrapped in a white cotton hand towel and says to have the time of our lives diving. "This is what you came so far for, right?" She winks.

Of course it is.

I suppose.

In Brisbane, we splurge and get six rolls of film developed. It's so expensive, as much as a week in a hostel, but we're flush and we can't wait any longer to look back.

There's a shot from JFK of my parents and Tracy's mom amid all the Taiwanese going home. There's our first tuk-tuk driver, and Christmas morning in Ko Samui, and Tracy buying bright gold mango chunks from a street vendor. Deeper in the envelopes are pictures from Kings Cross, Glebe Markets, Martin and his pal whose name I'm already unsure of—Jason? Justin?—Milly and John at Avoca, Pop in the yard holding lemons, Martin leaning into Captain Caveman, Evan in the art museum, floating in a corner of white floors, white walls, and white ceiling like a piece of abstract art waiting to be interpreted.

Finally, we get to the shot John took at the Sydney airport and my head's almost totally cut off. He focused on the kids in my arms. Perfect, really. That's exactly what I was: a pair of hands in a tough stretch.

I seal all the photos and negatives in a plastic bag and slide it deep in the pocket of my backpack, where I keep things I want to protect—immigration forms, traveler's checks, journals as they fill up, my plane ticket, the picture of my *Classic American* family, the best sculpture Milly Tanner ever made, and the photograph of Ellen Tanner that the kids let me take. It's nothing special. She's sitting by the pool with a magazine on her lap, lifeguarding Martin and Milly. They don't seem to know she's there, but that's impossible. Kids can always feel their mothers, right?

Children, Kelly. Goats have kids. Are they goats?

PART TWO

RETURNING

If I'd gone straight from the Tanners' house back to my mother's, I might have fallen into her and cried, confessing all the times I heard her talking as I walked from room to room on Lewiston Street, wishing I could call so she could tell me what to do. But I did not go back to her. I hitchhiked a thousand miles to resume my odyssey.

I rode a horse out of the rain forest, across a beach, and straight into the ocean. I stayed up all night to watch the sunrise in Gisborne, New Zealand, the place where every new day on earth begins. I bungee-jumped 129 feet off a bridge, first by myself and then tandem with Tracy, who wouldn't do it any other way. I scuba-dived a dozen times, mostly during the day but once at night, when it was dark and cold. In a postcard to my mom, I said it was like twirling through outer space with nothing but a flashlight, knowing full well that she would judge the exercise a colossal waste. I wandered around glaciers, fjords, and the lesser-known Fijian islands. I sang with a band and kissed many boys—eighteen, it says in my journal. And in all that manic doing, the curiosity about my mother that struck me so frequently at the Tanners' faded.

After reentering the United States through Los Angeles and driving across the country, I walked through the back door of

Wooded Lane on the afternoon of my parents' Christmas party, an event my mother hosted begrudgingly with my father, who never could understand why they didn't have people over more frequently, i.e., weekly.

She was standing at the sink rinsing dust off wineglasses. I stared at her, no longer sure what I was seeing: the actual woman or the woman I'd created in some unknowable mix of memory and imagination, and of longing.

We hugged. It was nice. She said my hair had gotten lighter and asked if I had lost weight. Then she looked at my scummy backpack on the floor and said, "You're not going to leave that there, are you?"

I sighed. "No, I guess not."

"Good, because you know wherever you put it, that's the first place someone is going to want to put their coat."

"Good to be home," I grumbled as I lifted the offending object.

"We'll get caught up tomorrow. You know your father. He has to have his big soiree."

That night, I passed hors d'oeuvres and emptied ashtrays. My dad pulled me close every time I passed. "Look at my girl! Can you believe it! My girl—a world traveler!"

At the kitchen table the next morning, I brought out the photos Tracy and I had developed in Brisbane.

"You have to go, Mom. Especially Australia. It's so awesome," I said, knowing *full damn well* that she'd probably never go to Mexico, much less *all the way the hell to Australia*.

My dad loved the verbal captions I made up for each shot. "Tell me more, Lovey!"

My mom pushed back from the table after about ten photos. She had seen enough. "The good news," she said as she rose, "is that you got home safe. Anything could have happened out there, Kelly."

Though I knew moving home would be fraught, there's only one place to unpack when you don't have a checking account or a phone number. My mom granted me the holidays to do my laundry, call all my friends, and drop the hint of Aussie intonation I had adopted. I spent most of my time writing letters to new friends back in New Zealand and Australia, people I would never see again, while watching game shows and soap operas. There was no reason to put on a bra or wear shoes. I usually waited until after lunch to brush my teeth.

After two such days—a day at home being such a long time, fourteen or fifteen hours from sunup to bedtime—my mother leaned in the doorway, appraised the value of my spending another afternoon on the sofa surrounded by aerograms and snapshots, and told me to make a list of every person I could call for work.

That took ten minutes.

"And go see your brother," she added.

GT was (and still is) a headhunter. I threw on my old duck boots and a Benetton sweater that went nearly to my knees.

"You may take the Buick," my mom said magnanimously, "but be back here by two P.M. I have a bridge match, against Overbrook no less."

GT lived across the street from Yang Ming, a Chinese restaurant unique for its formal atmosphere. He loved the dumplings. The moment I arrived, he called in a double order.

"I buy, you fly?" He held out a twenty.

"Sold." I dashed across Lancaster Avenue. Between a stack of take-out menus and the toothpick dispenser was a pile of xe-roxed job applications and a posted note that said: LUNCH SHIFTS ONLY. *Could be a nice way to break up the day,* I thought, and my mother would feel heeded. *Something's better than nothing,* she had said when I rejected her suggestion to do data entry for her friend's nonprofit inner-city tennis camp.

So this is how it happened that my first job back in the United States was as a coat check girl at Yang Ming. My opening shift, four hours, was midweek. The weather was terrible, welcome news for checkers of coats. The manager set me up on a folding chair in a closet behind a small counter with a tip jar pushed to the side. Every time I centered it, he tucked it back to the side.

The last customer left around three P.M. I had safeguarded twenty-seven coats and made, wait for it, three dollars. Three dollars. Trudging home down Lancaster Avenue, days of dirty snow in piles along the sidewalk, cars spraying slush on my new Payless flats, I talked to myself like a street drunk—*seventy-five fucking cents an hour*—about the staggering downturn in my fortunes since returning to my country. *A job,* I'd called it. *I got a job today,* I'd said.

"A month ago I was in Fiji!" I whined to my mom that evening. She laughed. She couldn't help it. Three bucks for four hours in a closet was *squarely in the funny category.*

Eventually, my old boss from the United Way in Baltimore tipped me off to an opening in the San Francisco office. After negotiating a relocation package, I packed up my red Jeep and grabbed my cousin Lisa and set out to drive back across the United States. I tried like hell to get Tracy to go with us, but she'd gone to work with her mom.

"God help the West Coast when you pull into town," my mother said, standing in the driveway, shaking her head. I'd be back east in a year, two max; that's what we thought. It would have been a different goodbye if we'd known I was leaving the East Coast forever.

I found an apartment on the corner of Franklin and Union and enrolled in grad school at night. I had my own office and health insurance. I quit smoking, along with everyone except the pierced-nose, roll-your-own-cigarette types from my master's program, who were more articulate and better read than anyone I'd ever met and who regarded me like I was overdressed and slightly off, like, say, Tipper Gore.

In a matter of months, my dad came out to visit. I threw a keg party for my new friends to meet him. The next day, we drove down to Palo Alto to watch the Fighting Irish crush Stanford. My mom did not come—not that weekend, not that year. Cross-country travel is *no casual thing,* and we were seeing each other back east for weddings *plenty*.

My roommate's mom came three times in the first year. After one of her visits, I said to my roommate, "I've been here for fourteen months, and my mother literally never even mentions coming. I mean, you'd think she'd want to see where her child was living." I wasn't afraid to phrase things dramatically; blame it on five months of *Santa Barbara*.

I wanted to take my mom to my office and introduce her to my manager, a strange and loving woman who fancied long fingernails, scarves, and dirty jokes. I wanted to take my mom for a burrito, surely her first, and show her all the fleeced boys in their hiking boots. I wanted to drive her across the Golden Gate Bridge with the top down.

"What does she say when you ask her?" my roommate said.

"Do I really have to ask her? I mean, don't parents just automatically—"

"I don't know. You're not, like, super-nice to her on the phone. Maybe she thinks you don't care."

I paused, then shook it off. "Oh, come on, that's crazy."

But the idea stayed with me, and the next time my mom called I asked her to come out, and she said she would look into it.

"She won't come, watch," I said to my roommate when I hung up.

Later that evening, she called me back with a choice of dates and flight times.

Applying her *Houseguests are like fish* rule, she came for three days. I took her to all the best places I had found to eat, to walk, to look. Pasta at i Fratelli, beers at Sam's, scones at Home Plate. The weather was perfect. She loved it.

Back at SFO on Monday morning, I walked her to the gate, as people did in 1994.

"You'll never come home," she said.

"Yes, I will—"

"No. If I'd seen this place when I was young, I'd have stayed forever."

It was hard for me to imagine my mother young. She'd never really been me, a girl out of college, looking at the map, wondering where to unpack her trunk and set up her JCPenney bedroom set.

"I'll be back, Ma. When it's time to buy a house . . ."

"No, it's too good here." She nodded, agreeing with herself, and then stepped into line at the ticket counter.

I never did come home to her, but I came around to her. It took ten years, two babies, and a tumor.

The first step was meeting a Yalie from Arkansas who had not traveled, did not do party tricks, and had never touched a lacrosse stick. We got married anyway, and though my mother was very happy with how the day turned out, the negotiations were tedious.

For example: "Now, have you thought about what kind of flowers you'd like on the tables?" my mom had asked the week after Edward proposed, using the officious and slightly obsequious tone of a wedding planner.

"I like gerbera daisies." My parents' wedding was a formal Catholic affair in early November. I memorized the album, each page its own black-and-white eight-by-ten. I can describe every shot, my mom's collarbones, my dad's buzz cut, the bridesmaids' velvet dresses, the groomsmen's wool morning suits.

"Gerbera daisies?"

"Gerbera daisies."

After a long pause, my mom said, "I was thinking roses."

"If you have it all figured out, why did you ask me what I wanted?"

"Because I thought you'd say roses and then I could agree and you'd think I'd given you exactly what you wanted."

We did the same dance with the venues. Church or hillside. Country club or Moose Lodge. In the end, it went exactly as both of us probably had known it would. St. Thomas of Villanova, Merion Golf Club.

After Edward and I came home from the honeymoon, I made a new list to work through. Some of the old favorites—lose weight, read the morning paper, run a 10K—mixed with some new and exciting items, like get pregnant, which happened fast because I am stupid lucky.

I went from wondering endlessly about mothers to becoming one over a slow and almost relaxing seventeen hours involving a delicious opiate called Fentanyl. Mothering Georgia has forced on me many decisions, and by many, of course I mean millions. The first big one was baptism. The issue had come up before, loosely during the pregnancy and intermittently since she was born. I'd been baptized, as had Edward. But did we believe enough to pass it on?

Though my mother loved invoking the adage *When you assume, you make an* ass *out of* u *and me,* she did indeed assume that Georgia would be baptized, as did Greenie. The alternative was unthinkable, a break in a chain that stretched back hundreds of years. Edward was inclined to defer to Pascal's Wager, the idea circulated by the French philosopher that if you believe in heaven and you're right, fantastic! All that virtuous living paid off. If you believe and you're wrong, well, hey, at least you spared yourself years of pride and sloth, not to mention killing, stealing, and bearing false witness.

My wager went: *Do it and your mother can die happy. Don't do it and break her heart forever.*

Many months later, when Georgia was practically walking, affairs were in order. We flew to Philadelphia to baptize her in the church where we were married.

The service was lovely and brief. Georgia wore a delicate lace and linen dress that Edward's parents sent from Little Rock. GT and Edward's sister, Phoebe, pledged to be good and wise godparents, and through it all I cried, surprising myself and Edward, who kept checking my expression to make sure I was crying happy tears. My mother, on the other hand, nodded at me as if she had seen this moment coming for thirty-four years.

I wasn't choked up thinking that Jesus knew my baby and that the Holy Spirit would guide her. It wasn't the marble altar or the brass crucifix hanging behind it that got me. I cried looking at my mom and realizing how much I had come to love her and how that love had brought us here to this chapel, where a hundred parishioners were promising to keep an eye out for her granddaughter, who would grow up in California and say the Lord's Prayer only when she was visiting her Jammy.

Pulling at the hem of my emotion was the creeping sense that it might well take until 2036 for this child in my arms to feel a fraction of what I already felt for her.

After Claire arrived, during a morning so grueling that when I think about it my lady parts clamp shut in an involuntary, sustained Kegel, we moved out of a rental flat in Berkeley and into a well-priced fixer-upper in a tiny suburb with very good public schools. My mom gave us a check to cover the last chunk of the deposit; she had plenty of money saved—*saying no adds up, Kelly*—and was no longer afraid I would spoil.

I played house, turning doors into chalkboards, making benches from plywood, sewing an ottoman slipcover that my mother-in-law joked, after a couple glasses of Pinot Grigio, "doesn't do your living room any favors." I started building my new life, collecting my own Pigeons for the road ahead. And I began the transition from my father's breezy relationship with the world to my mother's determined navigation of it.

At first parenthood was as I'd expected. Exhausting, sometimes heinous, occasionally divine. I held my children close enough to feel them breathe, laugh, swallow. Then my days got more complicated, and although there's nothing unusually challenging about my children, I often find myself responding to their sudden and inscrutable moods, mighty wills, and near-constant arguing by turning into a wild-eyed fishwife. Some interactions are so strangely familiar, it's as if I once starred as Little Orphan Annie and then, decades later, found myself cast in the revival as Miss Hannigan.

By way of example, here's a memorable excerpt from a conversation with Georgia regarding her third-grade report on cheetahs:

"You missed a section, honey."

"No, I didn't," she replies without looking.

"This page on reproduction is totally blank."

"I know. I Googled it, and there was nothing."

"Oh, I bet there are half a million pages about cheetah reproduction."

"Not on Google, not when I put it in the nav-bar thingy," she says, air-typing as if I'm new to the Internet and might need a little help following her.

"Maybe you spelled it wrong," I suggest in a gentle voice.

"I know how to spell *cheetah*. C-h-e—"

"I was thinking *reproduction*," I clarify.

"R-e-p—"

I smile even as her relentless contrariness boils my insides. "Okay, stop. When we go upstairs, I'll do it with you."

"But I did it already, and there are zero-point-zero sites," she says. I don't know which one of us is more fed up.

"I promise you there are many sites on the Internet that discuss cheetah reproduction," I say with great manufactured calm, trying a trick that involves pretending your child is not *your* child but, rather, just *a* child, *any* child, asking for your gentle guidance. Sometimes this works.

"There are no—" Sometimes it doesn't.

"STOP. That. Is. E-nough. E-NOUGH! Work on something else, but do not say one more word!"

"Fine."

After Georgia storms off, Edward says, "When I first met you, you didn't drink coffee, and you were so mellow." How can I tell him that I was a dog in show, high-stepping with my shiny hair and sparkly striped collar? Twelve years and two puppies later, I'm an ungroomed bitch who barks at flies.

Beneath my frustration is real fear. What if my kid lacks a handful of the critical Life Skills we're always reading about in the school newsletter: Persistence, Coachability, Curiosity? What if there's an iceberg hardening right now beneath this defeatism? If a child can't find a single word online about cheetah propagation, what kind of future can she hope for? That's why I snap and storm around and then spend long nights thinking of the most damaged adults I know and wondering if my particular brand of maternal fuckups are how they ended up like that.

My "passionate engagement" frees Edward from just about all worry. He sleeps fine. He talks to his friends about road bikes and tech start-ups and music apps. He stews about his job. Why should he fret about the girls when I'm pacing the sealant off the hardwood floors? It would be redundant.

Recently, he called with *good news!* We were invited up to Tahoe for four days with the O'Sullivans. "Our girls can ski with their girls, and we can have an adult day on the mountain."

This was a flawed plan, or at the very least a plan that required some consideration. Ten years into our marriage, I've learned to push back using Fact Not Feeling. "I thought we were in a period of post-Christmas austerity. Didn't you say we needed to get our *burn rate* back under control, build up the 529s, maybe pay down some of our mortgage . . ."

"Yes, but the place is free."

"Four days at Squaw equals sixteen lift tickets." I don't like being the family comptroller, but apparently it's a job that must be done.

"So are we just not going to ski, ever?"

The real problem with Freddy Fun's Tahoe plan was that the

O'Sullivan girls skied twenty days last winter, on double-black diamonds. Our girls are what the savvy ski schools call Advanced Beginners, which meant two things:

1. Without a parent to slow her down, Claire would hop off a ski lift and fly in whatever direction the slope took her, fly with her hands high and her skis tight together, fly until she met a tree or another skier or the cliff's edge. There was no helmet hard enough to protect her from her own recklessness.

2. Georgia, who does not like to be a beginner and will not ask for, or accept, help, would ride to the top of the mountain with the very able Maggie O and go wherever she led, even the Olympic runs, crying behind her ill-fitting loaner goggles, hating her inexperience and inferiority. Did Edward not know this? Could he not feel her insides clench like I could? God help them if anything ever happened to me.

"How are they going to learn if we don't let them try?" Edward wanted to know. "I don't want them to grow up scared of mountains and rivers and whatever else makes you nervous. I want them to be gamers, to be on the go team."

"Oh, come on—"

"Here I thought I married George Corrigan's daughter," Edward said, playing to my identity. "Don't tell me I married—"

"Watch it."

I'm not sure who Edward married. Maybe the person he married became a different person. Because maybe that different person is the right person for the job. Maybe *that* person will take on the cheetah report, and protect over- and underconfident children on ski slopes, and manage the unsettling situations that often bubble up right around bedtime.

One particularly tough night, I'd broken a wineglass while I was doing dishes, and Claire was still upset that I'd forgotten to take her down to the softball field that afternoon so she could be in the team picture, and my lower back ached, and let's just say the day was pleading to be done.

"Okay, girls, bedtime," I announced.

"I get to stay up longer," Georgia said.

"Why?" Claire asked.

"Because I'm two years older."

"Not for long," Claire said.

"Forever," Georgia replied, too casually for a truth so cruel.

"Nuh-uh. Someday I'll be nine."

"Right, but when you're nine, I'll be eleven." Claire's eyebrows knotted. "I will always be older than you," Georgia explained. Claire looked at me then at her sister, then back at me. Surely this was not the case.

"She's right, honey." This was as bad as anything I'd had to tell her over the years, as bad as Everything Dies. Even People. Even People You Know.

"Older," Georgia said, possibly ignorant of the existential magnitude. "Always and forever."

Claire made the face that preceded the noise that meant she was going to wail, and then it would be all over, because when she goes, she goes to 11.

"Georgia, please, stop!" I snapped. "She gets it, okay? You made your point."

"Why are you yelling at me?"

"I'm not!" I yelled. "Upstairs, bed, now."

"That's not fair!"

"Life's not fair."

I wrangled them into their rooms. As I closed Georgia's door, I heard Claire crying.

I leaned into her room. "What's the matter, Clairey?"

"Are you mad at Georgia?" she asked me.

"Yes. I'm frustrated. The bickering makes me crazy. And I've talked to Georgia—"

"What did you say?"

"The same thing I always say: Leave It Alone. Walk Away." She broke into a sob. "It's okay, Claire. I'm just saying—"

"It's not that!" she snapped, winding herself up in a way that racked me to watch.

"Claire, honey, what is it?" I readied myself for a confession. When she finally spoke, her voice was very small. "Do you love one of us more than the other?"

"No, do you think I do?"

"Yes!" she spat out, the deepest possible betrayal in her voice.

"You think I love Georgia more than I love you?"

"No," she sobbed, confusing me. "I think you love me more than you love Georgia!" To her mind, this was the most unforgivable treason; this violated a fundamental maternal vow.

Dropping off the girls the next morning, I looked for anyone I might be able to talk to about the night before. I ran into Beth and then Kristi, but I didn't know how to launch into the story, and I felt strangely self-conscious about Claire's concern, like I may have done something very wrong to surface such a fear. Besides, every mother on campus had her own problems. So I turned back toward Mountain Avenue and dialed my mom.

"Hey. So, did you—did we ever—okay, so Claire said the most disturbing thing last night. She said she thinks I love her more than I love Georgia. What am I supposed to do about *that*?"

"Well, I'll tell you," she started, "you do your damnedest to keep things even-Steven. And I mean everything: presents, sleepovers, eye contact. Your brothers once fought over tube socks. I'd put them in their stockings and GT ended up with an extra pair and I swear to God, it almost ruined Christmas."

"It's gonna be a long ten years."

"Ten? I *still* keep lists. Loans, visits, babysitting . . . You never stop tracking that one."

"Lovey!" My dad picked up the other phone.

"Hi, Greenie."

"Lovey! Great to hear your voice!"

While he told me about playing golf last week with Cousin Tommy and some other *youngsters,* I gnawed on the fact that in addition to helping the girls parse the world and all its awful truths—time goes only one way, things end, affections wax and wane—I was the sole distributor of the strongest currency they would ever know: maternal love.

It may be that loving children, radically and beyond reason, expands our capacity to love others, particularly our own mothers. A couple years ago, my mom volunteered (here she might say *agreed*) to keep the girls for five days and nights so I could tag along with Edward on a work trip to London. We would fly from California to Philadelphia, spend a couple of days settling the kids in at Wooded Lane, and then leave on the red-eye to Heathrow. I'd bought tickets to *Billy Elliot* and made a dinner reservation online at some bistro I read about in the *Times* travel section.

In preparation for our arrival, my mother was tidying up outside, pruning her impatiens. She wanted the patio to look nice as we sipped Inglenook over ice and ate Stoned Wheat Thins with Swiss while Greenie grilled burgers as big as softballs. While my mom was moving a wrought-iron serving tray on wheels, a rock she didn't see pushed the tray back into her shin, breaking the skin. She went upstairs to the tub to rinse out the cut, topping it with Neosporin, a favorite product of hers, and a large Band-Aid.

The morning of our arrival, a red ring had spread out from her cut, probably three or four inches in diameter. This worried exactly no one, least of all her.

"When you get old, everything takes twice as long to heal," my mom said.

We hung around the house that afternoon, the girls making lists of activities they wanted to do during the week. The Pigeons came by, one by one, to visit. Claire shared her newest set of riddles, and Georgia told them about her lacrosse coaches while the ladies snapped photos with their bad cameras and passed on clothes their granddaughters had outgrown.

After dinner, my mom took the girls up to the tub, squirting baby shampoo into the rush of water to make bubbles. Even though I was still there, my mother was in charge. After baths, she gave them each a two-minute back rub with the Flex targeted massager I bought years ago for her birthday in a panic at an airport Brookstone. All their bodily tensions released, the girls knelt by my mom's bed to say the Our Father and the Hail Mary. If that went well, my mom allowed them fifteen minutes of a *television program*.

Around seven P.M., MaryAnne popped by. After she hugged the girls and said how big and beautiful they looked, she caught sight of my mom's leg and gasped. "Mary! That's infected!" The ring was twice as big as it had been in the morning, and the swelling ran the length of her shin. "You need to take her to the hospital!" MaryAnne said to me, making me blush, ashamed that my mom's friend seemed more engaged in my mother's well-being than I was.

Within the hour, my mom had been seen by a general practitioner and sent from the ER to the third floor, where they started IV antibiotics. An infection had entered her bloodstream. The next morning, Edward went to the airport without me.

My mom's behavior in the hospital astonished me, the way a seasoned newscaster, usually so stern and unflappable, can shock you with a show of emotion.

She begged me to make them stop *all the poking*. Just getting the needle into her vein made her weep. *Look! Look at the bruises*. There was a nurse she thought wasn't listening to her. The original doctor, who she liked, had not come by again, and she wanted to make sure her case had not been transferred. A new doctor, who did not shake her hand or look her in the eye, said that if they were unable to get control of the infection, they would have to "at least consider" amputation. I could see, and damn near feel, the terror coursing through her.

I stood close to her and agreed with everything she said.

Those nurses *are* rough.

That bruising *is* crazy.

This food *could not be* more disgusting.

Whatever she felt, I felt with her. I did not try to dissuade her; I had learned that from my own Pigeon, Betsy. *It's our job to be on their side,* she told me, referring to both our children and our parents.

I sat by her side, making lists of things to bring from home: her special sleep shirt, a toothbrush, some underwear. The newspaper, a pencil for the crossword, her reading glasses.

When she got emotional, my father assured her, with uninformed optimism, that everything would be fine, while I asked the doctors hard questions and took notes. Our roles were set: my dad made the staff like us, I made them answer us. With my mom's powers disabled, I was the glue to his glitter.

When my mom slept, I flipped through the magazines I'd brought for her, and followed the ticker tape news along the bottom of the muted TV, and looked at her. She seemed old in the hospital bed, older than I was ready for, *at risk*. Her skin was thin, her cheeks and neck creped. Family life wore her down. The daily mash-up of tiny, stupid tasks, like roasting chickens and finding the other sneaker, crossed with monitoring rivalries and developing emotional circuitry and soothing when possible, all the while allowing some pockets of time to feel your own feelings and pursue your own pursuits—it's a lot to maneuver. But what compressed her into an old woman, what made her bones heavy and her joints stiff, what used her up, wasn't the labor. It was the bottomless worrying and wanting and hoping.

Even now, I realize, there's so much I'd like to know about this woman. What was she doing in the picture from the shore, in the maid's uniform, with the pot on her head? What does she say to God when she prays? Why did she fall in love with my dad? Was it because of his loud jolly bigness or despite it, or because there's some soft, quiet side of him I do not know? Did she end up telling him about my shoplifting—later that night, that year, ever? Why wasn't I allowed to have a blow dryer?

There's more, things I *need* to know. What do you do when kids play off each other? How do you stand their fits of hatred, the stomping and screaming and slamming? How do you let people talk about you, judge you, call you a witch? How do you know when to step in and when to recede? What am I doing wrong?

What does she need to know from me? Not much. Maybe she'd like to hear—much to my own surprise, not to mention Edward's—that I've ended up siding with her on many matters, especially matters involving parenting or, I should say, mothering.

There are no free-for-alls in my house; I'll hold back dessert, new jeans, a sleepover, anything at all, really, until I get whatever deliverable is due.

I'm not the kind of mother who lives a tourist's life in her own town, combing through the paper for festivals and nature walks and community potlucks.

I have never worked all week on a homemade Halloween costume, nor do I buy the girls dresses that require dry cleaning. A big treat is going to a secondhand clothing store and picking through the racks to see how much crap we can get for twenty dollars.

I insist on seat belts and bike helmets, even in the driveway. I tell my girls to be careful every time they leave the house, and I can't watch them climb a tree or walk through a parking lot without ripping off whatever bit of fingernail I can get between my teeth.

Many times, the high point of my day is after the house has been *mucked up* and I can take off my bra, pour some wine over ice, have a few nuts, and flip through the mail while the girls do their homework.

I don't give them false praise or cheap feedback, and the thought of my girls being rejected makes me more angry than sad. I read the notes I find in their pants pockets and the journals tucked in their dresser drawers. I fret over things long after Edward clicks off his reading light and goes to sleep—croup, melanoma, insecurity, precocious puberty. Raising people is not some lark. It's serious work with serious repercussions. It's air-traffic control. You can't step out for a minute; you can barely pause to scratch your ankle.

Eventually, after three days in the hospital, my mom looked over at me and said, "For God's sake, Kelly, go home and take a shower. I'm not dying." The antibiotics were clearly working. We could return to our usual ways. "And when you come back, bring the backgammon set and some chardonnay and the girls. Bring me my girls."

She doesn't need to hear any of this, but here I am, five years later, overflowing with things I want to say, more every day. And lucky me, she is still around to talk to. The trick is, she won't sit still for a lot of *blah-de-blah*. She knows I love her, appreciate her. She was *doing her job,* best she knew how, *and that's enough of that*.

It's not enough for me.

If she could stand it, I'd tell her that sometimes she can be pretty funny—in a Maggie Smith-ish way—and has a kind of grit I don't see in many other women. I'd tell her I'm no longer secretly trying to change her, to make her more outgoing or liberal or spendy.

I want her to know I have learned the difference between pampering and love, adventure and life experience, mothers and fathers.

I see now what she did for my dad and me, how she let our relationship stay simple and uncomplicated by drawing the fouls and taking the hits. It was her gift to me as a girl in the world, and I will give the same gift to my daughters.

I want her to know that I have seen how the light changes over the course of the day and I know that the rooms that start cold get warmer.

I'd tell her that I know now that there are no daughters who never embarrass, harass, dismiss, discount, deceive, neglect, baffle, appall, incite, or insult their mothers.

I want her to know that although I vote for Democrats and cry easily and still spend all my money going to places no one ever needs to go, I hate shopping and cooking and I have never used a douche. I live within my means and worship my girlfriends, especially the ones who play cards and rag me about keeping the thermostat set too low. I don't long for other mothers anymore; I don't even wonder about them. I was meant to be her daughter, and I consider it a damn good thing that she, of all people, was the principal agent in my development.

I want to tell my mom that I admire her, the quiet hero of 168 Wooded Lane, the way she marched head-on into each uncertain moment, changing as the circumstances demanded, like finding a good-paying job at forty-eight with three kids in college.

Even though I don't always know what she's talking about or why something bothers her or what's making her smile, it doesn't matter, I don't care anymore, I love her. It's like a good book: You don't have to be able to decode every passage to want to hug it when you finish.

Although I spend my Sunday mornings with *The New York Times* and a latte, I want her to know that sometimes, when I do go to church, I kneel in the pew and cry behind my hands. I don't know what that means, except I am overwhelmed with feeling, and that feeling has something to do with her.

I want her to know that I'll take care of her, even when it's not pretty or easy or cheap. Of course I will. The mother is the most essential piece on the board, the one you must protect. Only she has the range. Only she can move in multiple directions. Once she's gone, it's a whole different game.

Epilogue

Long ago, I lost touch with the Tanner family. John sent a letter shortly after I returned to the United States to say the kids were getting along quite well and that he'd been dating a nice woman. She had children of her own from a marriage that fell apart, and everyone got on. They were getting married. John and the kids had moved into her house, leaving Evan and Pop alone on Lewiston. Everything was good at Qantas. He didn't say if he had started doing theater again. I hoped he had.

In the past few years, I've tried to track them down through Facebook and LinkedIn. I found the house on Google Earth and came upon Pop's obituary, alongside a handsome photo of him in the prime of his life, when his daughter was alive.

I worked with a private investigator in Sydney to find John and the kids, but the voting records she sent did not show birth dates, and their real names are so common that every search yields hundreds of leads. Finally, this past year, I found Evan. He did not reply to my first email, or my second, or third, and I worried that it wasn't him, but eventually he wrote a short note saying hello and that he was so sorry to have made me wait and that I had his blessing to write about my experiences on Lewiston. He did not share contact information for John, Martin, or Milly. I can't begin to figure what would hold him back, but I have learned that we don't always know people as well as we think we do, as well as we want to.

I think about them.

Martin and his flamboyant, untimely joy. The first child to love me, to make me feel capable. The cheeky monkey. I wondered how long it took him to stop asking people what their mothers' names were and what all his boyish obsessions—pirates, Ninja Turtles, roly-poly bugs—gave way to. I wondered if he majored in marine biology so he could talk to Evan about oceans forever.

Milly, who was old enough to guard the door but young enough to watch *Beauty and the Beast* twice a week. I wondered if she ever ate PB&Js again and if she became as gorgeous as I guessed she would. I was glad she had someone to make Mother's Day treats for, even if it left her with a tinge of guilt. I hoped her stepmom did a decent job with the sex talk, and that she introduced the whole mess in a timely fashion. I used to think Milly might come find me in America, that I would pick her up at the airport, throw her backpack in the trunk, stare at her at every stoplight, looking for the girl whose hair I brushed. Mostly, though, I thought about how, all these years, twenty and counting, her mother never came back—not for graduation or a Sunday barbie, not to go for a walk or to split the last piece of pizza, not on Milly's hardest day, not on her best.

Evan, who I was just beginning to know. His needs had been deferred until Martin and Milly, first in the pecking order, were deemed stable, and to make matters worse, he was part of a different family, a family that had not operated as a unit in many years. I wondered if he ever got to grieve, full stop, flush out all the pain clinging to his insides, and then I wondered if that was even possible. I am still illiterate in the subject of loss.

I wondered what it was like when Evan finally moved out of the garage and into the house proper. Which room did he take—the master?—and how long did he live there? Did he stay on for years to help Pop die, burying him next to his daughter so Martin and Milly could visit both of them in one trip? Or did Pop make Evan fix his transmission and drive away, back to finish uni or to a new job as a park ranger on some mountain?

I saw online that he married, even after he saw close up how that sometimes turns out—divorce, death. I don't know if they have children but I imagined what it would be like to meet Evan's kids, turning them inside out by telling them that one spring I was a girl to him, a girl to kiss in the kitchen after midnight. Evan would ask whether I ever play chess or do the crossword—it would be the obvious small talk. *No, never,* I'd have to admit. *I reverted to myself.* We all go home. We all speak our first language forever.

And Ellen.

I thought of her first in 2004, when I found a lump in my breast, and again in the summer of 2006, when I had my ovaries removed, and finally, in the fall of 2007, on what I'm sure was the longest night of my life.

After thirty infusions and two surgeries, I'd had some champagne and returned to my regularly scheduled life, but six months later I rubbed up against something new and stony in my breast and went cold. When Edward got home that evening, he felt it, easily, and sent me over to see Emily Birenbaum, my OB friend, who gave me an exam on her sofa.

"Yeah, it's right here," she said, walking back and forth over the lump with her fingers. "It could be scar tissue . . . but I can't say. I'd get a biopsy appointment. Tomorrow, if you can." I emailed Susie Eder, my oncology nurse, and she wedged me into the morning schedule.

We went to bed, me in tears, Edward holding me from behind. He asked if he should cancel his business trip. I said no, just be back soon. There was no use in his staying home just to watch me get a biopsy. If I cried on the table, I had Susie Eder. And he'd be back before the results came, when the phone rang, and that was what mattered. There was no more talking.

After three appointments—exam, mammogram, fine-needle aspiration, the fastest way to biopsy a mass—I picked up the girls from school and took them over to Betsy's for dinner, where I drank three glasses of wine in half an hour. Although we referred to the tests, we didn't talk about them openly because we were not going to prelive it. I felt okay when I left her house, strong, but after the girls went to bed, I cried into my pillow like a teenager (or worse, like a grown woman). The road map I'd made on Outward Bound gave me until 2057, and though the next morning Susie Eder would set me free by saying No Tumor, Just Scar Tissue, that night, with my thumbs pushing on my new lump, I was sure the most awful thing was happening. All I could do to settle myself down was map out the future without me. Every mom I know has done this. All it takes is a jolt of turbulence on a plane or sliding across a patch of ice in your minivan.

I told myself that Edward and some merciful combination of nannies, teachers, coaches, and other people's mothers would take care of my girls. Beth would cook extra for them; she'd do it for a year without ever asking for permission. Betsy and Meg would take them to get fitted for bras and talk them through various dramas. Kim, Pam, and Sarah would edit their college essays until they rivaled any *New Yorker* piece. Tracy would invite them out to Fire Island and tell them stories she knows about me that other people don't. My parents would take them to church and go to their plays, games, recitals, and graduations. Booker would teach them how to tell a joke. GT would take them to Broadway shows and get them the best lacrosse sticks on Planet Earth. Together, my brothers and my parents, for as long as they lived, would make sure the girls knew that Corrigans were standing by, ready to show them a good time or keep their mother alive to them, whichever the situation required.

Then there was what I could do: make photo books to show them what our life together looked like, leave notes in their drawers that said, *Things happen when you leave the house!* and *Be awake to the possibilities!,* write letters about marriage and motherhood for Edward to give them on their big days, maybe record a video, jokey and light, just to be sure they could remember the sound of my voice saying nice things to them.

Somehow, like Martin and Milly, they would find a way forward.

I didn't worry so much about Edward, either. He would date again. Mary-Hope would set him up with newly divorced women from her office, and Mellie would scrutinize any companions he found on his own. My parents would try to hang back, but they'd have to sniff around, my mother less subtle than she imagines. Someone would find him and take him and love him, making for him an easy second act after an excruciating first. People do this all the time. They get on with it.

Even after imagining all this fineness—the girls (check), Edward (check)—I bawled, stuck on the awful thought that the reason I'd ended up in Ellen Tanner's house, the reason no one had hired me as a waitress or bartender, the reason I'd been fired by Eugenia Brown and answered an ad from a widower, was so I could see how a family goes on, so I could witness their suffering, their slow but indisputable survival.

That was how I knew I'd been crying for me. Because that's what I had learned, that it would be my loss above all. So there, in the darkest quietest deadest part of the night, I sent out the same prayer over and over again:

Please let me be here, in this house, with these people.

Please let me stay.

Because THIS IS IT. THIS IS THE GREAT ADVENTURE.

Acknowledgments

While having written a book is spectacular, actually writing a book, one word at a time, for sixty thousand words, is just god-awful. However, there is a considerable upside: discovering in your friends an impressive capacity for incisive analysis and carefully phrased "feedback." Before this book went to the professionals at Random House, whom I'll get to in a minute, it passed repeatedly among the hands of Sarah Handelsman, Phoebe Lichty, Pam Johann, Betsy Barnes, and the writer Kimberly Ford Chisholm. These are very smart women who had better things to do last year than push me up a mountain, but push me up they did. It is not an overstatement to say that without them I had no chance. Zero.

As for Random House, my lifeline there is Girl Wonder, Jen Smith, who has the enthusiastic mind of an Ivy League freshman and the patient wisdom of a seen-it-all granny. Jen worked through every round with me and then hand-delivered my finished pages to the powerhouse team of Libby McGuire, Jen Hershey, Allyson Pearl, Susan Corcoran, and Theresa Zoro, who rallied behind the book in a way I would not have dreamed possible (and I have elaborate, some say *delusional*, dreams). I love being a Random House author—it is an honor—and I have my whip-smart agent, Andrea Barzvi of Empire Library, to thank for placing me there. Andrea, it all comes down to you, and that long phone conversation in 2005. Thanks for calling me back. The first time, and every time. Is it beyond cheesy to say here that I love you? Maybe. But this is the one page of this book that is beyond the reach of an editor, so I'm leaving it in.

Finally, it's widely suspected—and I'm going to tell you now that it's true—that a writer on deadline is a wretched creature: moody, needy, distracted, weary. And so it is that I need to thank Edward and the girls, who did a fairly convincing job of pretending I wasn't (intermittently) insufferable these past few years. In the end, all my tap-dancing is for you, to make you smile, to make you proud, to make you think I'm cool.

About the Author

KELLY CORRIGAN is the author of *The Middle Place* and *Lift,* both *New York Times* bestsellers. She is also a contributor to *O, The Oprah Magazine, Good Housekeeping,* and Medium. Kelly co-founded Notes & Words, an annual benefit concert for Children's Oakland featuring writers and musicians on stage together. Her YouTube channel, which includes video essays like "Transcending" and interviews with writers like Michael Lewis and Anna Quindlen, has been viewed by millions. She lives in the Bay Area with her husband, Edward Lichty, their two daughters, and a poorly behaved chocolate lab, Hershey. You can find her essays, videos, and tour schedule at kellycorrigan.com.

About the Type

This book was set in Bembo, a typeface based on an old-style Roman face that was used for Cardinal Bembo's tract *De Aetna* in 1495. Bembo was cut by Francisco Griffo in the early sixteenth century. The Lanston Monotype Company of Philadelphia brought the well-proportioned letterforms of Bembo to the United States in the 1930s.